Flee from Heresy

Bishop Athanasius Schneider

Flee from Heresy

A Catholic Guide to Ancient and Modern Errors

SOPHIA INSTITUTE PRESS
Manchester, New Hampshire

Copyright © 2024 by Bishop Athanasius Schneider
Printed in the United States of America. All rights reserved.

Cover by Updatefordesign Studio

Cover image: Detail from the Ingeborg Psalter (ca. 1200), Ms. 66, fol. 56, provided in the public domain by The J. Paul Getty Museum, Los Angeles [99.MK.48.56]. Depicts the temptation to atheism, from the opening verse of Psalm 52: "The fool said in his heart: There is no God."

Bible quotations indicated with an asterisk (*) are either from the Challoner version of the Douay-Rheims Bible per the imprint of John Murphy Company (Baltimore, 1899), or the author's original translations from the Latin Vulgate; all others are taken from the Revised and New Revised Standard Version Bible: Catholic Edition, copyright © 1966, 1993 National Council of the Churches of Christ in the United States of America.

No part of this book may be reproduced, stored in a retrieval system, or transmitted in any form, or by any means, electronic, mechanical, photocopying, or otherwise, without the prior written permission of the publisher, except by a reviewer, who may quote brief passages in a review.

Sophia Institute Press
Box 5284, Manchester, NH 03108
1-800-888-9344
www.SophiaInstitute.com

Sophia Institute Press is a registered trademark of Sophia Institute.

paperback ISBN 979-8-88911-318-8

ebook ISBN 979-8-88911-319-5

Library of Congress Control Number: 2024937734

First printing

To Saint Athanasius, Bishop and Doctor of the Church, "true pillar of the Church, whose doctrine was the rule of the true faith,"[1] and "principal instrument, after the Apostles, by which the sacred truths of Christianity have been conveyed and secured to the world."[2]

---

[1] St. Gregory of Nazianzen, *Or.* 21.
[2] St. John Henry Newman, *Arians of the Fourth Century*, V:2.

*"Flee from these ungodly heresies;
for they are the inventions of the devil."*

St. Ignatius, Ad Trallianos, 10

"There must be also heresies: that they also, who are approved, may be made manifest among you."

1 Corinthians 11:19

Contents

PREFACE xiii

PART I
THE MYSTERY OF HERESY

Gravity of Heresy 5
Defining Heresy 6
Mystery of Heresy 7
How to Read This Book 9

PART II
TIMELINE OF DOCTRINAL ERRORS

Pre-Christian Era to the Present Time 13
1st CENTURY 18
2nd CENTURY 19
3rd CENTURY 22
4th CENTURY 24
5th CENTURY 28
6th CENTURY 29
7th CENTURY 29
8th and 9th CENTURIES 30
10th CENTURY 31
11th CENTURY 31
12th CENTURY 32

13th CENTURY 33
14th CENTURY 34
15th CENTURY 35
16th CENTURY 36
17th CENTURY 42
18th CENTURY 43
19th CENTURY 48
20th CENTURY 54
21st CENTURY 62

PART III
TOPICAL DISCUSSION OF ERRORS

Errors about God and the Trinity 67
Errors about the Creation 68
Errors about the Incarnation 75
Errors about the Redemption 78
Errors about the Church 81
Authority in the Church 93
Errors about Grace 107
Errors about Religious Liberty 111
Errors about the Sacraments 115
Errors about Morality 130
Errors about the Liturgy 156

PART IV
THE BLESSED VIRGIN MARY, DESTROYER OF HERESIES

Devotion to Mary, Destroyer of Heresies 165

APPENDIXES

Syllabus of Errors. 187
Syllabus Against the Modernists 203
Oath Against Modernism. 213
Declaration of Truths. 217

Index 235
About the Author. 257

PREFACE

Especially since the Middle Ages, many excellent books have offered a summary account of Christian doctrine, being generally referred to as "catechisms." Most of these have served to instruct and edify the members of the Catholic Church, as well as to better inform non-Catholics about the authentic teaching of Jesus Christ the Son of God—the doctrine preserved and passed on, whole and entire, in the Church alone. Our Lord assured us of this unchanging doctrinal integrity for all time, in speaking to His first apostles: "He that hears you, hears Me" (Lk 10:16).

As a Catholic bishop and successor of those first apostles, I have sought to add to this body of teaching manuscripts with my own work, *Credo: Compendium of the Catholic Faith* (Manchester: Sophia Institute Press, 2023). Since then, my travels and pastoral ministry have made it clear that there is need today for another book of a different kind, in which certain errors against the true Faith may be compiled and discussed, so that they may be more clearly recognized and avoided in our own time.

I have therefore composed the present work, *Flee from Heresy*, with three goals in mind: First, to console faithful Catholics in showing how heresies and other forms of religious error have been part of Church history since the first century; and that, like every form of evil, God has always used error to bring about some greater good in His mysterious providence. "All things work together unto good" (Rom 8:28). Second, to inform them about the more prominent and harmful errors that the Church has faced, ranging from the first century to our own time. It may come as a surprise to learn that many of today's errors have already been clearly addressed by the Church, often centuries ago. Third, to challenge them to better know, love, and pass on their Faith to others; for, "how shall they believe in Him, of Whom they have not heard?" (Rom 10:14*).

In composing this text, I have drawn upon several classic manuals of Church history and theology, as well as my own prior work in *Credo*. Unlike the more comprehensive treatment of Catholic doctrine in *Credo*, I have intentionally limited the considerations here to identifying errors of faith and morals in themselves: seeking to name and categorize these concisely, simply, and readably. I have therefore used the encyclopedic format alongside the catechetical method of question-and-answer, to serve readers of a wider range of ages and backgrounds. In this, I have been most grateful for the valuable help of Mr. Aaron Seng of the Catholic educational resource company Tradivox, and for the excellent publishing work of Sophia Institute Press.

It is my hope that, by clearly addressing past and present errors, Catholics will be better able to combat them in their own spheres of influence, embracing the changeless truths of divine revelation and leading others to the same. May the saints and angels intercede for all who will undertake this task, that they may "walk worthy of God, in all things pleasing; being fruitful in every good work, and increasing in the knowledge of God" (Col 1:10).

February 1, 2024, Feast of St. Ignatius of Antioch
✠ *Athanasius Schneider, Auxiliary Bishop of the Archdiocese of Saint Mary in Astana*

Flee from Heresy

Part I

The Mystery of Heresy

Gravity of Heresy

THE TRUE GRAVITY OF heresy cannot be understood apart from charity.

The one who truly loves, living by authentic charity, will combat whatever comes between him and the object of his love. The knight fights valiantly to save his bride, the mother protects her child, the soldier defends his homeland. Similarly, the soul that loves God will always seek to grow in deeper knowledge of Him, for "love follows knowledge"[3] — and yet, "how can he love God, whom he seeth not" (1 Jn 4:20), unless one truly knows God, through right doctrine and prayer?

Now, because all heresy is an obstacle to right knowledge of God, it hinders man's ability to fulfill the first and greatest commandment, the very purpose of our existence: to "love the Lord thy God, with thy whole heart, and with thy whole soul, and with thy whole mind, and with thy whole strength" (Mk 12:30). As such, those who truly love God will always oppose doctrinal error as among the greatest evils, "casting down imaginations, and every high thing that exalteth itself against the knowledge of God, and bringing into captivity every thought to the obedience of Christ" (2 Cor 10:5). St. Augustine maintains that this love and zeal for

---

[3] St. Thomas Aquinas, *Summa Theologiae* [ST] II-II, q. 27, a. 3, obj. 2.

right doctrine have characterized the true Church since the earliest days, and always will:

> The one Church, the true Church, the Catholic Church, is fighting against all heresies: fight, it can; be fought down, it cannot. As for heresies, they all went out of it, like unprofitable branches pruned from the vine; but it still abides in its root, in its Vine, in its charity. The gates of hell shall not prevail against it.[4]

Defining Heresy

The word *heresy* has been used in many ways throughout Church history; however, it has always been used to describe some form of choice or separation from a larger whole, coming from the Greek term *hairesis* ("selection, choice").

In the early Church, the term was used in a more general way, describing any idea that deviated from the authentic Christian teaching and practice of the apostles. In this sense, any error in faith or morals was a heresy, as was any group that happened to hold or practice such errors. As may be read in the writings of all the Church Fathers, heresy was regarded as one of the greatest of all evils.

> Polycarp regarded Marcion as the first-born of the Devil. Ignatius sees in heretics poisonous plants, or animals in human form. Justin and Tertullian condemn their errors as inspirations of the Evil One; Theophilus compares them to barren and rocky islands on which ships are wrecked; and

---

[4] St. Augustine, *De symbolo: Sermo ad catechumenos*, 14.

> Origen says, that as pirates place lights on cliffs to allure and destroy vessels in quest of refuge, so the Prince of this world lights the fires of false knowledge in order to destroy men. Jerome calls the congregations of the heretics synagogues of Satan (Ep. 123), and says their communion is to be avoided like that of vipers and scorpions. (Ep. 130)[5]

Eventually, the term *heresy* came to be understood more narrowly, as the rejection of truths of faith and morals only—things that must be believed in order to be considered a Catholic. In this narrower use of the term, all heresies are errors of some kind, but not all doctrinal errors are heresies.

Today, there are three basic uses of the term. First, any *proposition* which itself contradicts divine and Catholic faith is properly called a heresy, or "heretical." Second, the canonical *offense* of heresy is "the obstinate denial or doubt after the reception of baptism of some truth which is to be believed by divine and Catholic faith."[6] Third, the *mortal sin* of heresy is the offense of heresy, freely and knowingly committed by someone, which results in the complete loss of sanctifying grace in the soul—along with all virtues, all merits, and all hope of salvation, should a person die in that state.

Mystery of Heresy

It is among the greatest mysteries of divine providence that God should allow the evil of doctrinal error to ever afflict His Church.

---

[5] *The Catholic Encyclopedia* (New York: Robert Appleton Company, 1910), 7:259.

[6] Code of Canon Law, can. 751.

Although as an institution she is forever preserved free from error in her official teaching and binding commands, there are times when even her shepherds and teachers—the bishops, successors of the apostles—are permitted by God to fall into error, issuing faulty teachings or harmful commands in their ordinary ministry. God has even permitted some popes to affirm doctrinal errors and ambiguities in the past, while not being formal heresies as such. Such cases have been very rare, including Pope Honorius I (625–638), Pope John XXII (1316–1334), and Pope Francis (2013–). Certain affirmations in the texts of the Second Vatican Council (1962–1965), and in some statements of popes since then, have also lacked the necessary doctrinal precision and clarity, and are consequently open to misinterpretations.

Since apostolic times, this pattern has been variously repeated. In some of the most striking passages of the entire Bible, St. Paul prophesies: "Some shall depart from the faith, giving heed to spirits of error, and doctrines of devils" (1 Tm 4:1), and again, "I know that after my departure, ravening wolves will enter in among you [the bishops]... speaking perverse things, to draw away disciples after them" (Acts 20:29–30). It is only in his letter to the church at Corinth that St. Paul records the mysterious reasoning behind God's allowing for such evils in the midst of His beloved Church, even calling it a necessity: "There must be also heresies: that they also, who are approved, may be made manifest among you" (1 Corinthians 11:19).

In this, we learn that doctrinal error—like every other form of evil in our fallen world—is merely permitted by God for a good purpose: "That the trial of your faith (much more precious than gold which is tried by the fire) may be found unto praise and glory and honor at the appearing of Jesus Christ" (1 Pt 1:7). Indeed, the most terrible heresies and crisis periods in the Church's history have always led to greater precision and clarity in her official teaching, and to greater discipline and sanctity in her members.

In God's good time, doctrinal errors will always spur the members of the Church onward to a greater knowledge of Him and His works — and so, to greater love and holiness.

How to Read This Book

In this book, the term *heresy* is used in the older, broader sense of the term. Only some of the errors considered here are heresies in the proper, restricted sense given above; and nowhere is an individual or group deemed guilty of the *sin* of heresy (or any other sin). Rather, clear names and definitions have been assigned to certain ideas and systems of thought, identifying concepts that are inherently opposed to Catholic faith and morals at some level.

Tracing the history of ideas within human society is a complex discipline, and a complete account of every error that has affected the Church is obviously beyond the scope of this book. Instead, *Flee from Heresy* should be read as a kind of summary catalogue and brief discussion of certain errors, to better recognize and avoid the same. In short, this book serves as a road map for Catholics in heeding the advice of the great Father of the Church, St. Ignatius of Antioch: "Flee from these ungodly heresies; for they are the inventions of the devil."[7]

---

[7] *Ad Trallianos*, 10.

Part II

Timeline of Doctrinal Errors

WHILE NOT A COMPLETE account, the following list includes certain major errors that have faced the Church ever since its public manifestation at Pentecost. These errors have been roughly arranged by century, based on when they first appeared or became more prominent in public discourse. Occasionally, they are included according to the century in which their more notable proponents lived, and/or when a given error was formally condemned by the Church. For consistency, system names have been assigned whenever common or reasonable (e.g., Berengarianism rather than "Berengarius").

PRE-CHRISTIAN ERA TO THE PRESENT TIME

ANIMISM

Pantheistic system, believing that all things participate in divinity, and that objects, places, and creatures all possess a distinct spiritual essence. Animism perceives all things—animals, plants, rocks, rivers, weather systems, human handiworks, and in some cases, words themselves—as being animated, having agency and free will.

ATHEISM

From Greek *theos* ("God"), maintains that God does not exist, as opposed to any form of *theism*. In more recent times, atheism was promoted especially by German philosophers Ludwig Feuerbach (+1872), Karl Marx (+1883), and Friedrich Nietzsche (+1900), and took control of state organization in Bolshevik Soviet Communism, Albanian State Communism, Chinese State Communism (Maoism), and North Korean State Communism. Condemned by Pope Pius XI (+1939) in the Encyclical *Divini Redemptoris* (1937), and explicitly rejected at the Council of Vatican II (1962–1965).[8]

Determinism

Holds all actions and outcomes as predetermined by some inescapable governing force: fate (as in *fatalism*), celestial bodies (as in *astrology*), genetics (as in *biological determinism*), etc. Rejects the existence and possibility of free will—a tenet condemned by the Synod of Orange (529) and Council of Trent (1545–1563).[9]

Divination

Seeking knowledge of future events or hidden things by inadequate means and/or nondivine agencies.

Dualism

System positing two opposite and eternal principles in conflict—light and darkness, material and spiritual, good and evil. Generally holds the material universe and external acts as evil or morally neutral.

---

[8] See *Gaudium et Spes*, 19–21.
[9] See Session 6, can. 5.

GNOSTICISM

From the Greek *gnosis* ("knowledge"), maintains that salvation must be achieved through (often secret) initiation into some hidden knowledge; generally characterized by tenets of radical dualism, often opposing a "good god" and an "evil god" as co-eternal principles, with the "evil god" as creator of the visible material world, sexual diversification into male and female, and moral commandments (as in the Old Testament). The first anti-Gnostic writer was St. Justin Martyr (d. ca. 165). Fragments of St. Justin's anti-Gnostic treatise on the Resurrection (*Peri anastaseos*) are found in Methodius' *Dialogue on the Resurrection* and St. John Damascene's *Sacra Parellela*. The most important is the great anti-Gnostic work of St. Irenaeus, bishop of Lyon and Doctor of the Church (+202), called *Adversus Haereses*. The greatest anti-Gnostic controversialist of the early Church is Tertullian (+220), whose main anti-Gnostic works are *De Praescriptione haereticorum*, *Adversus Marcionem*, *Adversus Valentinianos*, *Scorpiace*, *De Carne Christi*, and *De Resurrectione Carnis*.

HEDONISM

Moral system holding pleasure as the norm of human conduct: achieving the maximum pleasure for the maximum number is its central ethic.

MAGIC

Seeking effects beyond the power of natural causes through nondivine agencies. When including secret ritual formulae, such practices are further known as *occultism*. When including dealings with demons, they are further known as *witchcraft*, *wizardry*, *sorcery*, and *shamanism*.

Monism

From Greek *monos* ("one"); denies discrete entities or real distinctions in the universe, holding that the apparently many are in fact only phases or manifestations of one singularity.

Paganism

In the broadest sense includes all religions other than the true one revealed by God, and, in a narrower sense, all those except for the major monotheistic systems of Christianity, Judaism, and Mohammedanism. The term is also sometimes used interchangeably with *polytheism*.

Pantheism

Maintains all things as participating in divinity. Rejects the distinction between the natural and supernatural, holding the universe as identical with and extensive of one supreme deity. The Church has repeatedly condemned the errors of pantheism. The *Syllabus Errorum* (1864) censured the notion that "There exists no Supreme, all-wise, all-provident Divine Being, distinct from the universe, and God is identical with the nature of things, and is, therefore, subject to changes. In effect, God is produced in man and in the world, and all things are God and have the very substance of God, and God is one and the same thing with the world, and, therefore, spirit with matter, necessity with liberty, good with evil, justice with injustice."[10] The Council of Vatican I (1869–1870) further anathematizes those who assert that the substance or essence of God and that of all things are one and the same, or that all things evolve from God's essence.[11]

---

[10] See I, 1; see also the entire *Syllabus Errorum* below.
[11] See Session 4, cann. 3–4.

Polytheism

Belief in many deities, occasionally subdivided by the number of deities professed: two deities as *bitheism*, three as *tritheism*, etc.

Reincarnationism

Holds that the same soul goes through several cycles of inhabiting different bodies. Also called *transmigrationism* and *metempsychosis*. Recently condemned by the International Theological Commission in *Some Current Questions in Eschatology* (1992),[12] and in the *Catechism of the Catholic Church* (1992).[13]

Satanism (Diabolism, Demonism)

Religious worship of Satan and/or other demons, or whatever the practitioner perceives as opposed to God.

Spiritism

Belief that men can and do communicate with departed souls, or any attempt to practice such communication. When such practices contain a devotional religious aspect (as in ancestor-worship), it is known as *necromancy*. Modern Spiritism or *Kardecism* originated in France with teacher Allan Kardec (+1869), who claimed to combine scientific, philosophical, and religious aspects in his doctrine "founded on the existence, manifestations, and teachings of spirits." Adherents are widely known for promoting social assistance and philanthropy, with a strong influence on various other religious currents such as Santería, Umbanda, and New Age. Spiritism and its various practices have been condemned by the Congregation of

---

[12] See especially 9.3.
[13] See 1013.

the Inquisition in 1840, 1847, and 1856, with various Spiritist works proscribed by the Index in 1864. The Synod of Baltimore II (1866) and a later decree of the Holy Office (March 30, 1898) also condemned the movement.

TOTEMISM

Animistic system in which a certain individual or group holds some form of mystical identification with a discrete material object or class of objects.

1st CENTURY

DOCETISM

From the Greek *dokein* ("to seem"); maintains the humanity of Jesus Christ as partly or entirely illusory; i.e., Our Lord only seemed to be a man, or only seemed to have been born, lived, suffered, or died. This heresy, which destroys the very meaning and purpose of the Incarnation, was combated even by the Apostles. St. Paul's statement that in Christ dwelt the fullness of the Godhead bodily (cf. Col 1:19, 2:9) may refer to Docetist errors, and St. John undoubtedly refers to this heresy (see 1 Jn 1:1–3, 4:1–3; 2 Jn 7). In sub-apostolic times this sect was vigorously combated by St. Ignatius (+107) and St. Polycarp (+156), with the former warning against Docetists as "monsters in human shape" (see also his Letters: to the Trallians 10; Ephesians 7 and 18; Smyrnaeans 1–6). Tertullian wrote a treatise *On the Flesh of Christ* and attacked Docetic errors in his *Adversus Marcionem*. Hippolytus (+235) refutes Docetism in his *Philosophoumena*, among several other Gnostic errors.

JUDAIZING

Holds the Mosaic Law and/or ceremonies as morally binding (e.g., rest and worship on Saturday rather than Sunday, ritual circumcision, washing, and dietary laws) and/or able to communicate grace in themselves, without reference to or faith in Jesus Christ. Condemned by the Council of the Apostles in Jerusalem (ca. 50–51). St. Ignatius of Antioch still warns against Judaizers in the early second century,[14] as the Judaizing movement divided into three main sects: 1) the *Nazarenes*, who, while still observing the Mosaic Law, seem to have been orthodox in admitting the divinity of Christ and virgin birth; 2) the *Ebionites*, who denied the divinity of Christ and virgin birth, and considered St. Paul an apostate; 3) an Ebionite offshoot infected with Gnosticism.

2ND CENTURY

ADOPTIONISM

Broad category for Christological theories according to which Christ, as man, is not the natural but only the adoptive Son of God. Propounded by the Roman merchant Theodotus of Byzantium (ca. 190), later revived by bishop Paul of Samosata (+275). Theodotus was excommunicated by Pope Victor (+197), and Paul of Samosata was condemned by the Synod of Antioch (268).

BASILIDEANISM

Named for Gnostic teacher Basilides of Alexandria (+138); holds an evolutionary account of man's origin and the evil of the material

---

[14] See *Magnes*, 10:3; 8:1; *Philad*, 6:1.

cosmos, which must be escaped to attain spiritual disembodiment and salvation.

MARCIONISM

Named for founder Marcion (+160) of Paphlagonia, an ancient region on the Black Sea coast of north-central Anatolia; holds the God of the Old Testament to be a secondary deity or demiurge, substantially different from the loving God of the New Testament. Rapidly drifted into Gnosticism. In the Platonic, Neopythagorean, Middle Platonic, and Neoplatonic schools of philosophy, the *demiurge* is a certain deified figure responsible for fashioning and maintaining the physical universe—a notion widely adopted by the Gnostics. Several Church Fathers and Ecclesiastical Writers condemned Marcionism, e.g. Tertullian (+240) in *Adversus Marcionem*.

MODALISM

From Latin *modus* ("mode"); belief that the Father, Son, and Holy Spirit are not separate and distinct divine persons, but simply three modes or manifestations of one and the same divine being. Also known as Sabellianism and *Patripassianism* ("father-suffering") for holding that God the Father became incarnate in Christ and sacrificed Himself on the cross, or that in the sufferings of Jesus Christ, God the Father also suffered. Modalism was first formally stated by the priest Noetus of Smyrna (ca. 190), and further developed by the priest Sabellius (ca. 210). Noetus was condemned by the Bishop of Smyrna, Tertullian wrote *Adversus Praxeam* against this tenet, and Sabellius was condemned in 220 by Pope Callistus (+222).

MONARCHIANISM

Any Christian heresy rejecting the Trinitarian nature of God in various ways; subdivided as Adoptionism and Modalism.

MONTANISM

Named for Gnostic founder Montanus (d. latter half of the second century) of Asia Minor; emphasizes personal enlightenment, prophetic utterance, ecstatic experience, and ongoing public revelation through the inspired founders. Also known as *Phrygianism* (for Phrygia, its region of origin in Asia Minor), *Cataphrygianism* ("from Phrygia"), and *Pepuzianism* (after the town of Pepuza, which adherents regarded as the "new Jerusalem"). The churches of Asia Minor excommunicated Montanists around 177, and bishop Apollinarius of Hierapolis presided over a synod which condemned Montanism.

VALENTINIANISM

Named for Gnostic founder Valentinus of Alexandria (+180); maintains an elaborate pantheistic system of creation and existence emanating from a supreme being, with salvation available only through true knowledge of universal principles. Condemned especially by: St. Irenaeus of Lyon (+202) in *Adversus haereses*,[15] Hippolytus in *Philosophumena*,[16] and Tertullian in *Adversus Valentinianos*.

---

[15] See I, 1; III, 4.
[16] See VI, 20–37.

3rd CENTURY

Adoptionism

Monarchian system, maintaining that Jesus Christ was not the Son of God from all eternity, but was supernaturally adopted by God the Father during His earthly life. Formally condemned by Pope Damasus I (+384) in the *Tomus Damasi* issued by the Roman Synod in 382.[17]

Apokatastasis

Universalist system expecting a future in which all free creatures will share in the grace of eternal salvation—in a special way, the devils and condemned souls in hell. Condemned at the local Synod of Constantinople (543), and anathematized at the Council of Constantinople II (553).

Manichaeism

Named for Gnostic founder Mani from Persia (+277); a popular synthesis of several world religions under a dualistic system of "pure reason" and salvation through knowledge. Manichaeism was rejected by St. Ephraem (+373) in his treatise against the Manichaeans, published in the form of poems from 59 to 73. St. Epiphanius bishop of Salamis (+403) devoted his great work *Adversus Haereses* (ca. 374) mainly to refuting Manichaeism. The greatest opponent of Manichaeism was St. Augustine, bishop of Hippo (+430); see the works *De utilitate credendi, De moribus Manichaeorum, De duabus animabus, Contra Fortunatum, De actis*

---

[17] See can. 6.

cum Felice, De Natura Boni, Contra Secundinum, and *Contra Adversarium Legis et Prophetarum.*

Novatianism

Named for Roman priest Novatian (+258), antipope from 251 to 258; denies the power of the Church to remit sins in certain cases, particularly in granting absolution to Catholics who lapsed during the early Church persecutions. Novatian was excommunicated by Pope Cornelius (+253) at a 251 synod in Rome, and Novatianism was condemned by the Council of Nicea I (325).[18]

Origenism

Certain doctrines rightly or wrongly attributed to the Alexandrian priest Origen (+232), especially: the preexistence of all souls—i.e., God originally created innumerable disembodied souls, who later sinned and fell, becoming embodied as demons, people, and angels in accordance with the degree of their fall—and a universalist notion of salvation, also called *apokatastasis*. Pope Anastasius I (+401) condemned several doctrinal errors in Origen's work *De Principiis* in 401, while the Synod of Constantinople issued fifteen anathemas against specific doctrines of Origen, which were in turn approved by Pope Vigilius (+555) and all the Oriental Patriarchs.

Rebaptism

Custom in Africa and Asia Minor of rebaptizing converts from heresy. Pope St. Stephen (+257) absolutely condemned the practice, commanding that converted heretics receive only the imposition of hands for the sake of penance, since the baptism conferred by

---

[18] See can. 8.

heretics or schismatics was held as valid according to primitive custom—St. Augustine (+430) believing this to be an apostolic tradition, and St. Vincent of Lérins (+445) holding rebaptism as contrary to the rule of the universal Church.

4TH CENTURY

APOLLINARIANISM

Named for bishop Apollinaris of Laodicea (+382); maintains that Jesus Christ possessed a human body, but did not have a human mind or soul. Eagerness to emphasize the full divinity of the Son of God and the unity of his person led Apollinaris to deny the existence of a rational human soul in Christ's human nature. Condemned by Pope Damasus I (+384) in a Letter to the Oriental Bishops (374), and declared to be a heresy by the Council of Constantinople I (381).

ARIANISM

Named for heresiarch priest Arius of Alexandria (+336); major heresy denying that the Son is of one essence, nature, or substance with God the Father. Holds the Son as not consubstantial (*homoousios*) with the Father, being therefore not like Him, nor equal in dignity, nor co-eternal, nor truly God—rather, holds the Son as only an excellent being (created, not eternally begotten) and that therefore, there was time when the Son of God did not exist. Arius was first condemned as a heretic at the Council of Nicea I (325), and Arianism was finally condemned by the Council of Constantinople I (381).

Donatism

Named for bishop Donatus of Casae Nigrae in North Africa (+355); maintains complete moral integrity as necessary for priestly ministry and valid sacraments; led to a schism that endured into the sixth century. First condemned by the Synod of Arles (314), confirmed by Pope Silvester I (+335). St. Augustine rejected *Donatism* in several of his works, e.g. *Contra epistolam Parmeniani, De Baptismo contra Donatistas, Contra litteras Petiliani*. Significant is also the great work of St. Optatus, bishop of Milevis in North Africa (d. late fourth century), *De schismate Donatistarum*.

Eunomianism (Anomoeanism, Heteroousianism)

Named for bishop Eunomius of Cyzicus (+393) in northwest ancient Asia Minor; Arianist system holding the Son as *anhomoios* ("unlike") the Father in substance and all else, as opposed to the *homoousios* ("of the same substance") maintained by the true and traditional faith, confirmed at the Council of Nicea I (325). Opposed even the *homoiousios* ("of similar substance") of the Semi-Arians, and the later *homoios* ("resembling") of the Acacians. Condemned by Pope Damasus I (+384) in the *Tomus Damasi* issued by the Roman Synod in 382.[19]

Homoianism (Acacianism)

Arian system rejecting the consubstantiality of the Son with the Father as defined by the Council of Nicea I (325); holds the Son of God as only similar (*homoios*) to the Father, without reference to His substance (essence). Also called *Acacianism* for its major proponent, bishop Acacius of Caesarea (+366). Dominated the

---

[19] See can. 6.

Church during much of the fourth-century Arian Controversy. Condemned by Pope Damasus I in the *Tomus Damasi* issued by the Roman Synod in 382.[20]

HOMOIOUSIANISM (SEMI-ARIANISM)

Held by many Oriental bishops during the Arian Controversy; maintains the Son of God as only similar in substance (*homoiousios*) to the Father, but not equal in substance (*homoousios*) as the Council of Nicea I (325) defined. Various iterations range from true orthodoxy under different phrasing (due to misunderstandings of *homoousios*) to disguised Arianism under more moderate terms.

JOVINIANISM

Named for monk Jovinian (+405); opposes asceticism, rejects the ontological superiority of virginity, denies the ability to sin for the baptized, rejects the perpetual virginity of Mary. Condemned at a 390 synod in Rome under Pope Siricius (+399), and subsequently at a synod convened at Milan by St. Ambrose (+397). St. Jerome wrote against this heresy in *Adversus Jovinianum* (392), and St. Augustine opposed it in *De sancta virginitate* (401).

MACEDONIANISM

Named for bishop Macedonius of Constantinople (+361); rejects the divinity of the Holy Spirit. Adherents also called Pneumatomachians ("Spirit-fighters"). Condemned at the Council of Constantinople I (381).

---

[20] See can. 6.

MELETIANISM

Named for bishop Melitius of Lycopolis in Egypt (+327); form of Donatism leading to schism that lasted to the eighth century. Meletius was deposed in 306 by a synod in Alexandria.

MONOPHYSITISM (MONOPHYSISM)

Maintains that Jesus Christ has only one nature, resulting from His divine nature having completely absorbed His human nature. Later called *Eutychianism* after its major proponent, archimandrite Eutyches of Constantinople (+456). Eutyches was excommunicated in 448, with monophysitism and Eutyches both condemned at the Council of Chalcedon (451).

PRISCILLIANISM

Gnostic-Manichaen sect developed in the Iberian Peninsula by bishop Priscillian of Avila (+385), holding matter and nature as evil. Practiced extreme asceticism, fasting on Sundays and Christmas Day, and held esoteric doctrines with the belief that most could not understand the "higher paths"; adherents were thus permitted to tell lies for a holy purpose. Condemned by the Synod of Zaragoza (380), and its members excommunicated.

SUBORDINATIONISM

Any Christian heresy rejecting the eternal and divine coequality of the Son and/or the Holy Spirit with the Father; maintaining the former as somehow subordinate to the Father in nature or operation, or both. Posits a hierarchical ranking of the persons of the Trinity, implying ontological subordination within the Trinity of the persons of the Son and the Holy Spirit. Arianism developed out of this concept.

5th Century

Nestorianism

Named for bishop Nestorius of Constantinople (+451); maintains two distinct persons in Jesus Christ, denying that the Son of God was born, suffered, or died on the cross, and consequently rejects the title *theotokos* ("Mother of God") for the Blessed Virgin Mary. Condemned at the Council of Ephesus I (431) and again at the Council of Chalcedon (451).

Pelagianism

Named for Romano-British monk and theologian Pelagius (+418); denies original sin and the necessity of divine grace for salvation. Pelagianism was first condemned in 416 by the North African Synods of Carthage and Mileve, and confirmed in 417 by Pope Innocent I (+417). In 418 Pope Zosimus (+418) excommunicated Pelagius. The condemnations of Pelagianism were finally confirmed at the Council of Ephesus (431).

Predestinarianism

Term for various Christian heresies that deny man's free cooperation with grace as a secondary cause of his own salvation, reducing all salvation or damnation to the single cause of God's sovereign will.

6th Century

Semi-Pelagianism

Doctrine of grace advocated by monks of Southern Gaul in the late fifth and early sixth centuries; aimed at compromising between Pelagianism and Augustinism, it was condemned as heresy at the Council of Orange (529). Adherents also known as *Massilians* ("those from Marseille") or *reliquiae Pelagianorum* ("relics of the Pelagians"[21]). St. Augustine fought against this heresy mainly in these works: *De gratia et libero arbitrio, De correptione et gratia, De praedestinatione sanctorum, De dono perseverantiae.*

7th Century

Monothelitism

Modified form of monophysitism, holding only one principle of intention and will, and only one kind of activity or operation (*energeia*) in Christ. Personhood held as manifest in will and action, so that a single personality must involve a single will and activity; the Person of Christ, therefore, could only have one divino-human will and one divino-human activity. First condemned by Pope Martin I (+655) at the Lateran Synod (649), and later at the Council of Constantinople III (680–681).

---

[21] See St. Augustine, *Ep.* 225, 7.

Paulicianism

Founded by one Constantine of Armenia, possibly named for one Paul who led the sect's migration to North Anatolia after its persecution by Emperor Justinian II (+711) in the late seventh century. Accepted the four Gospels, fourteen Epistles of Paul, the three Epistles of John, James, and Jude, and a purported Epistle to the Laodiceans. Rejected the Old Testament and the title of "Mother of God," refusing to venerate the Virgin Mary or the cross, which was held as a pagan symbol. Believed Christ to have come to emancipate men from the body and the world, which were seen as evil. Rejected outward administration of the sacraments of the Lord's Supper and baptism.

8th and 9th Centuries

Iconoclasm (Iconomachy)

From the Greek *eikonoklasmos* ("image-breaking"); belief that the veneration of God by way of sacred images (icons) constitutes idolatry, often encouraging the destruction of such images. Condemned by the Council of Nicea II (787).

Spanish Adoptionism

Adoptionist system appearing in eighth-century Spain, asserting a double sonship in Christ: one by generation and nature, and the other by adoption and grace. Christ *as God* is held as the Son of God by generation and nature, but Christ *as man* is the Son of God only by adoption and grace. "The Man Christ" is therefore the adoptive, but not the natural, Son of God. Taught by Archbishop

Elipandus of Toledo (+805), suggesting that Christ's human nature existed separately from His divine personhood—a nuanced form of Nestorianism. Elipandus' teaching was condemned in 785 as heresy by Pope Hadrian I (+795), and again by the Councils of Ratisbon (792) and Frankfurt (794).

10TH CENTURY

Bogomilism
A neo-Gnostic, dualist sect founded in the First Bulgarian Empire by the priest Bogomil; mitigated-dualism system known for rejecting marriage, war, capital punishment, oaths, private wealth, and institutional authority.

Tondrakianism
Named for the Armenian district of Tondrak, north of Lake Van; Gnostic system especially known for rejecting apostolic succession, Church authority, and the immortality of the soul. Flourished in medieval Armenia from the early ninth to the eleventh century.

11TH CENTURY

Berengarianism
Named for archdeacon Berengarius of Tours (+1088); maintains a merely spiritual or figurative presence of Jesus Christ in the Eucharist. First condemned by a synod in Rome in 1050, then by several other local synods.

Eastern Orthodoxy

From the Great (East-West) Schism of 1054; denies the revealed truth of papal primacy and the supreme authority of the Roman See.

Nominalism

From the Latin *nomen* ("name"); philosophical system denying the existence of abstract or universal concepts, and/or the power of the intellect to create or perceive them. Maintains only sensible particulars in space and time as real or describable, with concepts only existing as verbal labels for collections of things. An early proponent of Nominalism was the French theologian Roscellinus (+1125), with Nominalist ideas also present in the work of French theologian Peter Abelard (+1142) and English Franciscan theologian William of Ockham (+1347).

12th CENTURY

Catharism (Albigensianism)

From the Greek *katharos* ("pure"), adherents sometimes referred to as Albigensians, after the French city Albi where the movement first took hold; general term for several neo-Manichean sects of the middle ages, especially known for the many bloody wars it engendered. Opposed to both Church and State authority, advocating for the renunciation of marriage and ritual suicide to attain liberation from the material world. Formally condemned by the Council of Lateran IV (1215).[22]

---

[22] See *Definitio contra Albigenses et Catharos*.

PETROBRUSIANISM

Named for French priest Peter of Bruys (+1131). He opposed infant baptism, erecting of churches, veneration of crosses, the doctrine of transubstantiation, and prayers for the dead. Condemned by the Council of Lateran II (1139).[23]

WALDENSIANISM

Named for founder Peter Waldo (+1217); originally known as the "Poor of Lyon" in the late twelfth century, the movement spread to southeast France and north Italy. Peter Waldo, a wealthy merchant, gave away his property around 1173, preaching apostolic poverty as the way to perfection. He rejected the doctrine of purgatory, indulgences, prayer for the dead, and ecclesiastical authority. In the sixteenth century, the Waldensians were absorbed into the Protestant movement. Waldo was excommunicated by Pope Lucius III (+1185) in a synod at Verona in 1184. In 1208 Pope Innocent III (+1216) required a detailed profession of faith from the Waldensians (*Professio fidei Waldensibus praescripta*).

13TH CENTURY

AMALRICISM

Named for priest Amalricus de Bène (+1207); pantheist system denying transubstantiation, confounding good and evil, and claiming the incarnation of God the Father in Abraham. Considered by Martin Luther to be a proto-Protestantism. First condemned by a synod at Paris in 1210, and then at the Council of Lateran IV (1215).

---

[23] See cann. 22, 23.

Fraticelli

Term for various sects related in some way to the medieval mendicant orders of consecrated religious, predominantly the Franciscans. Stressed asceticism, personal piety, and evangelical poverty, frequently unto the denial of ecclesiastical authority, private property, and the created goodness of the material world. Condemned by Pope John XXII (+1334) in the Bull *Gloriosam Ecclesiam* (1318).

Joachimism

Named for Joachim of Fiore (+1202), a Cistercian monk and later Benedictine abbot in south Italy; holds three states of the world and dispensations of grace, in which the third "age of the Holy Spirit" was to dawn in utopian bliss about the year 1260. Later followers of Joachim's eschatology and historicist theories were called Joachimites, and some of his ideas about the nature of the Trinity were condemned at the Council of Lateran IV (1215).

Neo-Adamism

Term for various sects venerating the biblical Adam and claiming to regain man's original innocence; frequently practiced nudity, promiscuity, and sharing of goods amongst the community (a kind of "communism").

14th Century

Hussitism

A Czech proto-Protestant movement following the teachings of the priest Jan Hus (+1415); a recapitulation of Wycliffism in Bohemia, leading to the Hussite Wars (1419–1434). The errors of Hus were condemned by the Council of Constance in 1415.[24]

WYCLIFFISM

Named for English priest John Wycliff (+1384); anticipation of later Protestantism in rejecting the government of the Church, papal supremacy, transubstantiation, and the sacramental system, also advocating for the subjection of church property to the civil prince. In England, also called *Lollardism* from the Latin *lollium* (a "tare") in the mid-fourteenth to the fifteenth century; having become not only a scholastic issue and violently anti-clerical but also propagandist and heretical, in 1382 a council in London condemned twenty-four of Wycliff's "Conclusions" — ten as heresies, fourteen as "errors." The errors of Wycliff were condemned by the Council of Constance (1414–1418).[25]

15TH CENTURY

CONCILIARISM

Theory that a general or ecumenical council of the Church is higher in authority than the pope. Began in the fourteenth century with William of Ockham (+1349) in his battle with Pope John XXII (+1334), questioning the divine institution of the primacy. Marsilius of Padua (+1324) and John of Jandun (+1324) declared this was only a primacy of honor, and during the great Western Schism (1378–1417) many otherwise reputable theologians, such as Peter

---

[24] See Session 15.
[25] See Session 8.

of Ailly (+1420) and John Gerson (+1429), saw in the doctrine of the council's superiority over the pope the only means of again reuniting a divided Church. The fourth and fifth sessions of the Council of Constance (1414–1418) declared the superiority of a council over a pope, but these propositions never received papal approbation. Conciliarism was first condemned by Pope Pius II (+1464) in the Bull *Exsecrabilis* (1460), and definitively corrected at the Council of Vatican I (1869–1870).

16TH CENTURY

ANABAPTISM

Particularly radical Protestant system originating in Germany in the early 1500s, rejects infant baptism and State authority, initially endeavoring to found a communist social order. Meaning "one who baptizes again," Anabaptists were so called for baptizing those who converted or declared their faith in Christ, even if they had already been baptized as infants. Erroneously interpreting the Sermon on the Mount (Mt 5–7), they rejected all use of force or military action, and discouraged participation in civil government. Anabaptist practice was condemned by the Council of Trent (1545–1563).[26]

ANGLICANISM

The beliefs and position of members of the established Church of England, and of its communicating churches in British territories, the United States (where it is called the *Episcopal Church*), and elsewhere. Its doctrine is mostly Calvinist, though retaining a

---

[26] See *Decree on Original Sin*, Session 5.

hierarchical constitution (deacon, presbyter-bishop) and some classical liturgical elements. Maintains the English monarch is the supreme head of the Church of England, and claims to have apostolic succession; however, Pope Leo XIII (+1903) declared Anglican orders invalid in the Apostolic Letter *Apostolicae Curae* (1896). The Bible is accepted as the sole and supreme rule of faith, while much latitude is allowed as to the nature and extent of its inspiration. Eucharistic teaching is subject to various and opposed interpretations. Apostolic succession is held as beneficial but not essential to the nature of the Church. The Apostles' Creed is the only one to which assent can be required. Loyalty to the Protestant character of the Anglican Church has produced the *Evangelical* or *Low Church* school of Anglicanism; a rationalist focus is found in the *Latitudinarian* or *Broad Church* school of Anglicanism; and higher and philocatholic views about Church authority, belief, and worship are seen in the *High Church* school, especially in the Oxford or Tractarian Movement of the nineteenth century.

Antinomianism

Neo-Gnostic tenet holding Christians as exempt from the external obligations of the moral law. First attributed to Johannes Agricola (+1566), who stated: "If you sin, be happy, it should have no consequence." Condemned by the Council of Trent (1545–1563).[27]

Baianism

Named for the Belgian priest Michael Baius (+1589); pseudo-Protestant system denying the supernatural character of man's original justice, maintains man's total corruption through sin and

---

[27] See *Decree on Justification*, Session 6, chap. 15.

his justification as a merely moral rehabilitation. It is a curious mixture of Catholic orthodoxy and tendencies to Protestantism, and may be seen as a precursor to Jansenism. Main errors condemned by Pope Pius V (+1572) in the Bull *Ex omnibus afflictionibus* (1567), and definitively condemned by Pope Gregory XIII (+1585) in the Bull *Provisionis nostrae* (1579).

CALVINISM

Named for the French teacher John Calvin (+1564); Protestant system, stresses man's total depravity and *predestination*. Holds God as having appointed the eternal destiny of some to salvation by grace, while leaving the remainder to receive eternal damnation for their sins, even original sin. John Calvin taught a double predestination: that God offers salvation to some, but not to all. His doctrines were condemned by the Council of Trent (1545–1563).[28]

ILLUMINISM (ALUMBRADOS)

From the Latin *illuminare* ("enlighten"), the name *illuminati* (*alumbrados* in Spanish) was assumed by some false mystics who appeared in Spain in the sixteenth century, claiming to have direct intercourse with God; holds that the human soul can reach such perfection in this life as to directly contemplate the divine essence and comprehend the mystery of the Trinity. All external worship is held as superfluous, the reception of the sacraments useless, and sin impossible in this state of complete union with Him Who is Perfection Itself. Carnal desires may likewise be indulged, and other sinful actions committed freely, without staining the soul. The highest perfection attainable by the Christian consists in the elimination

---

[28] See *Decree on Justification*, Session 6, cann. 15, 17.

of all personal activity, loss of individuality, and complete absorption in God. Maintained until the middle of the seventeenth century, with some features reappearing in the Quietism of Spanish priest Miguel de Molinos (+1696).

LUTHERANISM

Named for German priest and Augustinian monk Martin Luther (+1546); religious system held by the oldest and most numerous of the Protestant sects in Europe. "Lutheran" was first used by Luther's opponents during the Leipzig Disputation (1519) and afterwards became a universal designation, although Luther preferred "Evangelical," so that the contemporary title is often *Evangelical Lutheran Church*. In Germany, where the Lutherans and the Reformed have united since 1817, the name *Lutheran* has been abandoned, and they are known as the *Evangelical* or the *Evangelical United Church*. Classical Lutheranism professed a so-called "sacramental union" between the Body of Christ and the substance of bread, in the well-known formula: The Body of Christ is in, with, and under the bread (*in, cum, et sub pane*) really present, though only at the moment of its reception by the faithful (*in usu, non extra usum*). In attacking Lutherans, Reformed theologians (Zwingli, Calvin) called this doctrine *impanation*. Luther was condemned in 1520 by Pope Leo X (+1521) and excommunicated in 1521, with his doctrines condemned by the Council of Trent (1545–1563).

PROBABILISM

Moral system first introduced in 1577 by Spanish Dominican theologian Bartolomé Medina (+1580); holds that freedom may be exercised as soon as a corresponding opinion is well-founded, even if the opposite opinion would be objectively better founded and provide more moral certainty. Viewed by solid Catholic theologians as an easy road to moral *Laxism,* since people often regard opinions as probable that are based on flimsy arguments; instead, objective Catholic morals are stressed by rejecting opinions which lead to Laxism. In 1762, St. Alphonsus de Liguori (named the patron of confessors and moral theologians by Pope Pius XII in 1950) openly and formally abandoned the opinion of Probabilism.

PROTESTANTISM

General term for innumerable Christian sects maintaining fundamental separation from Catholicism concerning the rule of faith, means of justification, and constitution of the Church. The term derives from the German Lutheran princes' protest letter of 1529 against an edict of the Diet of Speyer that condemned the teachings of Martin Luther as heretical. Most Protestant systems maintain justification by faith alone, and Scripture as the sole rule of faith, while rejecting most Catholic doctrines on the hierarchical structure of the Church, papal primacy, the number and nature of the sacraments, and especially the dogmas of transubstantiation, the sacrificial character of the Mass, consecrated celibacy, purgatory, prayer for the dead, indulgences, and the veneration of saints and holy images. The various doctrines of Protestantism were first condemned by the Council of Trent (1545–1563).

SOCINIANISM

Named for Italian Renaissance humanist and theologian Fausto Sozzini (+1604) and his uncle Lelio Sozzini (+1562), co-founders of a "non-trinitarian Christian" movement; pseudo-Protestant system rejecting the Trinity, Incarnation, Redemption, original sin, justification, infant baptism, and all but two (merely symbolic) sacraments. This heresy was condemned by Pope Pius IV (+1565) in the Bull *Cum quorumdam hominem* (1555).

UNITARIANISM

Affirms the singular nature and personhood of God as the one and unique creator of the universe; believes that Jesus Christ was divinely inspired in His moral teachings and that He is the savior of humankind, but denies that He and the Holy Spirit are also divine Persons co-equal with God, hence rejecting faith in the Most Holy Trinity. The earliest known Unitarian Christian denomination was the Unitarian Church of Transylvania, founded by preacher and theologian Ferenc Dávid (+1579). *Unitarian* is now applied to those belonging to a Unitarian church but who do not always hold a Unitarian theology, while in the past, most members of Unitarian churches were also Unitarian in theology; e.g., in the 1890s, the American Unitarian Association began admitting even non-Christian and non-theistic churches and individuals.

ZWINGLIANISM

Named for Swiss priest Ulrich (Huldrich) Zwingli (+1531); Protestant system, stresses Scripture and private judgment in matters of faith. Regarding the Eucharist, Zwingli said that after the Ascension, the body of Jesus was to be found only in Heaven, and thus could not be really present in earthly bread. He claimed that the so-called "consecrated" bread was not the Body of Jesus, but merely a symbol of it; accordingly, the *est* ("is") of Christ's institution of the Eucharist (see Mt 26:25–29; Mk 14:22–25; Lk 22:19–23) must be understood only in a figurative sense. His doctrines were condemned by the Council of Trent (1545–1563).

17th CENTURY

JANSENISM

Named for the Dutch bishop Cornelius Jansen of Ypres in Flanders (+1638), holds God's commands as impossible to observe in certain cases, that interior grace is impossible to resist, and that salvation is nowise merited by man's free acts; characterized by moral and sacramental rigorism. One typical Jansenist affirmation was that Christ did not die for all men. First condemned by Pope Innocent X (+1655) in the Bull *Cum occasione* (1653). Pope Clement XI (+1721) confirmed the condemnation in the Bull *Vineam Domini* (1705), and proscribed other Jansenist errors in the Bull *Unigenitus* (1713). Pope Pius VI (+1799) condemned various Jansenist tenets and practices in the Apostolic Constitution *Auctorem Fidei* (1794).

LAXISM

Moral system based on probabilism; maintains that if a less-safe opinion is slightly probable, it may be followed with a good conscience. In practice, promotes moral permissiveness leading to moral relativism. The principal upholders of this view were the French Jesuit Étienne Bauny (+1649) and the Italian Jesuit Tommaso Tamburini (+1675). Condemned by Pope Alexander VII (+1667) in 1665 and 1666, and expressly by Pope Innocent XI (+1689) in 1679, censuring various propositions which "savored of Laxism."

QUIETISM

From the Latin *quies, quietus* ("passivity"), a sort of false or exaggerated mysticism which broadly holds man's highest perfection as consisting in a sort of self-annihilation and absorption of the soul into the Divine Essence even during earthly life; in such "quietude" the mind is wholly inactive, no longer thinking or willing, but passive while God acts within it. Under the guise of lofty spirituality, it contains erroneous notions undermining objective morality. It is fostered by pantheism and similar theories involving peculiar notions about Divine cooperation in human acts. In the strict sense, Quietism is the doctrine also called *Molinism,* named for the Spanish priest Miguel de Molinos (+1696). From this developed the less radical *Semiquietism,* whose principal advocates were French bishop François Fénelon (+1715) and Madame Guyon (+1717). All these varieties of Quietism affirm interior passivity as the essential condition of perfection, and all have been condemned by the Church. Pope Innocent XI (+1689) condemned the Quietist errors of Molinos in the Bull *Coelestis Pastor* (1687).

18TH CENTURY

Agnosticism

From the Greek *a-gnostikos* ("unknown"), position of methodical doubt of the intellect's ability to know, or about certain things that can be known. Especially attributed to the system of theological uncertainty about God's existence, holding that human reason is incapable of providing sufficient rational grounds to justify either the belief that God exists or that He does not exist. Condemned by Pope Pius X (+1914) in the Encyclical *Pascendi Dominici Gregis* (1907).[29]

[29] See 6.

Deism

From the Latin *Deus* ("God"), generally agnostic system viewing God as an impersonal force of origin, unconcerned or unable to intervene in history; tends to rationalism and naturalism. Rejects revelation as a source of divine knowledge and asserts that empirical reason and observation of the natural world are the exclusively logical, reliable, and sufficient means for determining the existence of a Supreme Being. In its inception, a central premise of Deism was that contemporary religions were corruptions of one original, pure, natural, simple, and rational religion. Promotes reason and freethought, arguing against institutionalized religions in general and the Christian doctrine in particular. The best-known proponents of Deism were English philosopher David Hume (+1776) and United States' founders Thomas Jefferson (+1826) and Thomas Paine (+1809). Deism is a central ideological pillar of Freemasonry. The errors of Deism were anathemized by the Council of Vatican I (1869–1870) in the Dogmatic Constitution *Dei Filius*.[30]

Enlightenment Anthropocentrism

General shift to a human-centric philosophy and moral system; for religion this entails a change from considering divinely revealed dogmas, morals, and forms of worship, to a merely natural and historically conditioned view of religions as personally and/or socially beneficial constructs.

Episcopalism

System denying the universal jurisdiction and primacy of the pope, viewing him as "first among equals," one bishop among others,

---

[30] See *De revelatione*, can. 2.

with individual bishops as supreme in their own sees. Episcopalism found its practical expression in Gallicanism, Febronianism, and Josephinism. The most notable manifestation of Episcopalism was the Synod of Pistoia (1786). The Council of Vatican I (1869–1870) condemned the various tendencies of Episcopalism.[31]

FEBRONIANISM

Politico-ecclesiastical system of bishop Johann Nikolaus von Hontheim of Trier (+1790) under the pseudonym *Justinus Febronius*; Gallicanist in principle, developing a theory of ecclesiastical organization founded on a denial of the monarchical constitution of the Church, with the ostensible purpose of reconciling Protestant bodies with the Church. Condemned by Pope Pius VI (+1799) in the Brief *Super soliditate petrae* (1786).

FREEMASONRY

Hermetically closed, secret, and elitist Neo-Gnostic sect of the so-called "elect," "illuminated," or "initiated ones" in contrast to the rest of humanity, which is considered as "profane." It originated formally in 1717 in London. The most common disguise with which Freemasonry camouflages itself is beneficence and philanthropy, proposing a universal naturalistic religion: a mixture of pantheism, gnosis, and "self-salvation" based on the naturalistic fraternity of the bonds of blood and nature. The fundamental ideological pillar is thereby Deism, the categorical rejection of Divine Revelation. The essence of the Masonic religion consists of the perversion, that is, of the subversion of the divine order of creation and of the transgression of the laws given by God. Higher-degree Masons see in this perversion the "true

---

[31] See Session 4, chap. 3.

progress" of humanity, the mental building of the "temple of humanity." Instead of God's revelation, there stands the "Masonic secret," and the human being ultimately makes himself a god. Freemasonry is, therefore, a complete Anti-Church, where all the theological and moral foundations of the Catholic Church are turned into their opposite. First condemned by Pope Clement XII (+1740) in the Bull *In eminenti apostolates specula* (1738), followed by the Apostolic Constitution *Providas Romanorum* (1751) of Pope Benedict XIV (+1758). The most comprehensive condemnation of Freemasonry was made in the 1884 Encyclical *Humanum Genus* of Pope Leo XIII (+1903). The most recent judgments of the Church on Freemasonry were *The Declaration on Masonic Associations* (1983) approved by Pope John Paul II (+2005), and *Ex Audientia Sanctissimi* (2023) approved by Pope Francis, maintaining the Church's condemnation of Masonic associations and reaffirmation that Catholics are forbidden from joining Freemasonry, because the Church has always considered Masonic principles irreconcilable with her doctrine.

Gallicanism

General term for religious opinions once peculiar to the Church of France, or Gallican Church; tends chiefly to a restraint of the pope's authority in the Church in favor of that of the bishops and temporal rulers, subjecting papal Magisterium and jurisdiction to the power of the State, approval of local Churches, and/or conciliar decree. The historical antecedents of Gallicanism are seen in the French government's 1438 "Pragmatic Sanction of Bourges," which contains tenets of the supremacy of an ecumenical council over the pope, and of the limitation of his power. Gallicanism was systematically codified in the "Declaration of the Clergy of France," a 1681 document of the assembled French clergy condemned by Pope Alexander VIII (+1691) in the Bull *Inter multiplices* (1690).

JOSEPHINISM

Named for Holy Roman Emperor Joseph II (+1790); a Gallicanist, Febronian, and Freemasonic ideology imposed on Austria. Treated ecclesiastical institutions as public departments of the State, preventing bishops from communicating directly with the Roman Curia. Dissolved five hundred of the Empire's 1,188 monasteries, as Joseph II was virulently opposed to contemplative cloistered religious life and heavily influenced by the famous Freemason Voltaire (+1778), whose real name was François-Marie Arouet.

METHODISM

Also called *Wesleyanism* for founder John Wesley (+1791), Protestant system emphasizing practical Christianity over doctrinal orthodoxy, commending good works while denying their necessity for salvation.

NATURALISM

General term for systems holding the observable order of nature as the extent of all reality, denying all transcendence and supernatural realities, and seeking to explain everything exclusively in terms of the observable. Naturalism was condemned by Pope Pius IX (+1878) in the Encyclical *Quanta cura* (1864) and the *Syllabus Errorum* (1864).[32]

---

[32] See I, 1–7.

QUESNELLISM

Named for French priest Pasquier Quesnel (+1719); Baianist-Jansenist system especially attacking the Roman primacy. Formally condemned by Pope Clement XI (+1721) in the Bull *Unigenitus Dei Filius* (1713), condemning 101 specific errors.

RATIONALISM

General term for (especially Protestant) moral and theological systems in which human reason is deemed the primary if not the exclusive source and measure of truth. Postulates a religion of "pure reason" with moralizing tendencies, in the axiom that reason recognizes no judge over itself—constructing and worshipping a God made in man's own "image and likeness." Condemned by Pope Pius IX (+1878) in the Encyclical *Qui pluribus* (1846), and the *Syllabus Errorum*.[33]

19TH CENTURY

AMERICANISM

General term for certain teachings condemned by Pope Leo XIII (+1903) in his Apostolic Letter *Testem Benevolentiae* (1899): the rejection of external spiritual direction as no longer necessary, the extolling of natural over supernatural virtues, the preference of active over passive virtues, the rejection of religious vows as incompatible with Christian liberty, and the adoption of a new method of apologetics and approach to non-Catholics—i.e., in the Church adapting herself to modern civilization and relaxing

---

[33] Ibid.

her ancient moral and doctrinal rigor, to make converts by passing over or minimizing certain points of doctrine, or even giving them a meaning which the Church has never held.

BRANCH THEORY

Theological concept within Anglicanism, principally from Oxford scholar William Palmer (+1885); holds that the Roman Catholic Church, the Eastern Orthodox Churches, and the Anglican Communion are three principal branches of the One, Holy, Catholic, and Apostolic Church. This theory was condemned by the Holy See in a Letter of the Holy Office (September 16, 1864).

COMMUNISM

Socioeconomic system largely based on the theories of Karl Marx (+1883) and Friedrich Engels (+1895). Contrary to natural law, it denies the right to private property and undermines the social order itself, being historically used to promote materialism, atheism, and systematic persecution of the Church or its complete marginalization in social and public life. Communism, based on the Marxist ideology, leads to a totalitarian society. Formally condemned by Popes Pius IX (+1878) in 1846, Leo XIII (+1903) in 1878, and Pius XI (+1939) in 1937.

DARWINISM

Named for proponent Charles Darwin (+1882), general term for pseudo-scientific theories of human origins as formation over countless ages of random and gradual development, generally called *human evolution*.

Fideism (Traditionalism)

Philosophical-theological theory which holds authority as the only rule of certitude, which has its ultimate foundation in divine revelation, reserved and transmitted in all ages through society and manifested by tradition (*traditio*), common sense, or some other agent of a social character. Maintained by French philosopher Louis de Bonald (+1840), who laid great stress on tradition within society as the means of transmitting revelation and the criterion of certitude; by the French philosopher Augustin Bonnetty (+1879), who accepted the possibility of contradictions between faith and reason, with man's certitude of God's existence coming through faith alone; by French priest Louis-Eugene-Marie Bautain (+1867), who claimed divine revelation as the only source of knowledge and certitude. Men should be moved to faith by interior experience or private revelation. Moderate Fideism (sometimes called *Traditionalism*) maintains that human reason alone is unable to know the fundamental truths of the moral and religious orders, but can demonstrate the reasonableness of faith after accepting the teaching of revelation concerning them. The various errors of Fideism (Traditionalism) were condemned by Pope Gregory XVI (+1846) in 1840 and 1844, by obliging Bautain to accept the true Catholic theses on these points. The errors of Bonnetty were condemned by the Congregation of the Index in 1855, and the Council of Vatican I anathematized the main principles of Fideism (Traditionalism).[34]

Latitudinarianism

Theory originating in seventeenth-century Anglicanism, that the essential doctrines of Christianity are summed up in a few great,

---

[34] See Dogmatic Constitution *Dei Filius*, chap. 3, can. 3.

simple truths which are clearly expressed in Scripture, and that whoever believes these and regulates his life accordingly is a true follower of Christ; consequently, it makes little difference to what particular "Christian denomination" one adheres. This theory was condemned by Pope Pius IX (+1878) in the *Syllabus Errorum* (1864).[35]

Marxism

Named for proponent Karl Marx (+1883); general term for systems of socioeconomic organization promoting the abolishment of private property in favor of shared or public control of human goods, services, and activities. Often used interchangeably with *communism* and *socialism*. Core elements include "class struggle" as the fundamental law of history, total subordination of the person to the collective, and the myth of a proletarian class, invested with its mission in history—all to imply violence rather than love as the foundation of social order, by which is shown its fundamental opposition to Christianity.

Materialism

Naturalist system maintaining empirically observable matter as all that exists; rejects the purely spiritual, holding mind and consciousness as by-products of material processes, and all that exists as ultimately physical. Ludwig Feuerbach (+1872) introduced anthropological materialism, which views materialist anthropology as the universal science. Karl Marx (+1883) and Friedrich Engels (+1895) extended the concept of materialism to elaborate a materialist conception of history, called "Dialectical Materialism." Pope Pius IX (+1878) condemned Materialism in the *Syllabus Errorum* (1864),[36]

---

[35] See III, 15–18.
[36] See VII, 58.

the Council of Vatican I (1869–1870) anathematized Materialism,[37] and "Dialectical Materialism" was condemned by Pius XII (+1958) in the Encyclical *Humani generis* (1950).

Mormonism

Named for the *Book of Mormon*, central religious text by American author Joseph Smith (+1844), founder of the Church of Jesus Christ of Latter-Day Saints; neo-Gnostic system, rejects the Trinity, original sin, and Christian baptism, while justifying and promoting polygamy.

Positivism

In philosophy, a materialist and naturalist system; in theology, a deist or pantheist view of God and nature; in law, holds only the express tenets of written law as binding and supreme. Modern positivism was first stated by French philosopher Auguste Comte (+1857).

Religious Indifferentism

Rejection of the notion that there is only one true religion, or that man has any moral duty to know and practice it. It views all forms of religion as equal and fundamentally denies all categories of "true" and "false" regarding religion. It was condemned first by Pope Leo XII (+1829) in the Encyclical *Ubi primum* (1824), then by Pope Gregory XVI (+1846) in the Encyclical *Mirari vos* (1832), and by Pope Pius IX (+1878) in the *Syllabus Errorum* (1864).[38]

---

[37] See Dogmatic Constitution *Dei Filius, De Deo rerum omnium creatore*, can. 2.
[38] See III, 15–18.

SEMIRATIONALISM: HERMESIAN SYSTEM

Named for German priest Georg Hermes (+1831), who propagated a rationalistic conception of the idea of revelation itself; holding the principle of theology as not only methodical doubt, but positive doubt. This system holds that consent to faith is not free, but must be brought about through arguments of human reason. This system leads to skepticism and indifferentism. Condemned by Pope Gregory XVI (+1846) in the Brief *Dum acerbissimas* (1835), and by the Council of Vatican I (1869–1870).[39]

SEMIRATIONALISM: GUENTHERIAN SYSTEM

Named for Austrian priest Anton Günther (+1863), who held that revealed truths are only supernatural in a relative sense, and should gradually turn into truths of reason; even the proper mysteries of the Trinity and Incarnation can be understood scientifically. Therefore, the doctrine of faith could be reformulated as science advances. Semirationalism devolves into a religious belief in science. Günther's theories were condemned in 1857 by the Holy Office, and by Pope Pius IX (+1878) in the Brief *Eximiam tuam* (1857).

SOCIALISM

Economic and political philosophy centered on common ownership and the material welfare of society, to the detriment of private property and religious life. Condemned by Pope Pius IX (+1878) in the Encyclical *Quanta cura* (1864). Founded on a notion of human society which holds no objective beyond material well-being (see Pope John XXIII, Encyclical *Mater et Magistra* [1961]), *religious socialism* and *Christian socialism* are therefore

---

[39] See Dogmatic Constitution *Dei Filius*, chap. 3, can. 5.

contradictory phrases. A socialist concept of society is antithetical to Christian truth, as affirmed by Pope Pius XI (see Encyclical *Quadragesimo Anno* [1931]).

20TH CENTURY

ACTIVISM (HERESY OF ACTION)

Approach to personal and social activity not based upon the help of grace, nor seeking constant use of the means necessary to pursue sanctity given by Christ; gives religious primacy to temporal virtues and external actions (often for social benefit) over the supernatural realities of grace, prayer, and the interior life of holiness. Assumes that the world can be saved through social action unsupported by grace. Condemned especially by Pope Leo XIII (+1903) in the Apostolic Letter *Testem Benevolentiae* (1899) and Pope Pius XII (+1958) in the Apostolic Exhortation *Menti Nostrae* (1950).

ANTHROPOCENTRISM

From the Greek *anthropos* ("man") and *kentron* ("center"), holds human existence as the primary end of creation, and his social flourishing as the ultimate moral concern. Anthropocentrism's most dangerous form appears when man puts himself in the place of God, contemning God's majesty and, as it were, making the world into a temple wherein he himself is to be adored. Anthropocentrism creates a corrupting paganism. Condemned by Pope Pius X (+1914) in the Encyclical *E Supremi* (1903), and by Pope Pius XII (+1958) in the Encyclical *Summi Pontificatus* (1939). A distorted form of anthropocentrism has become a feature of the Modernist movement within the Church, in which love and service of God are reduced to love and service of humankind. The first commandment, "You must love the Lord your God with all your heart," is thus transformed into the second commandment: "You must love your neighbor," which then becomes not the second but the only commandment.

BALTHASARIANISM

Named for Swiss priest Hans Urs von Balthasar (+1988), entertains hope for universal salvation, and that hell is empty.

CONSEQUENTIALISM, PROPORTIONALISM

Moral systems in which intentions and/or situational outcomes determine the moral value of actions; "the end justifies the means." *Consequentialism* locates the moral rightness of an action solely in calculating the foreseeable outcomes of a given choice. *Proportionalism* is differentiated by weighing the various values and goods being sought and their means, focusing on the proportionality of the "greater good" or "lesser evil" achievable in a given situation. Both systems destroy the notion of any action being wrong in itself (*intrinsece malum*, "intrinsically evil") simply due to the kind of action it is (e.g., murder, blasphemy), apart from all possible outcomes or intentions. Condemned by Pope John Paul II (+2005) in the Encyclical *Veritatis Splendor* (1993).[40]

EXISTENTIALISM

Philosophical system generally held as originating with Danish philosopher Søren Kierkegaard (+1855); the first proponent to identify with the term was French philosopher Jean-Paul Sartre (+1980),

---

[40] See 75–76.

who held that all existentialists have in common the fundamental doctrine that "existence precedes essence," thus inverting the principle of perennial philosophy which says that existence and action follow essence/being (*agere sequitur esse*). Existentialism says that human beings, through their own consciousness, create their own values and determine the meaning of their life. With no objective meaning in the world, this leads to radical subjectivism on all levels, and the world becomes marked by absurdity. Other representatives of this philosophy were the German Martin Heidegger (+1976) and the French Albert Camus (+1960). Pope Pius XII (+1958) condemned Existentialism in his Encyclical *Humani generis* (1950).

False Ecumenism (Irenism)

The theory and practice that searches for a Christian unity that does not yet exist, as if Christ has not already conferred this perfect unity upon His true Church. One of its basic tenets holds that what unites Catholics to separated Christian communities is greater than that which separates them, undermining thereby the unicity of the Catholic Church and promoting doctrinal relativism. Such Ecumenism was condemned by Pope Pius XI (+1939) in the Encyclical *Mortalium animos* (1928) and by Pope Pius XII (+1958) in the Encyclical *Humani generis* (1950).

Feminism

Sociopolitical advocacy for the supposed equality of the sexes, tending to the destruction of natural distinction and proper roles in marriage, family, and society. Rejected in the Letter of the Congregation for the Doctrine of the Faith *On the Collaboration of Men and Women in the Church and the World* (2004).

Gradualism

Notion of "gradualness" in law, as if there were different degrees or forms of precept for various individuals and situations; proportionalist moral system in which one's general intention to conform to natural or divine law justifies direct individual acts contrary to the same. The erroneous theory of "gradualness of the law" cannot be identified with "the law of gradualness," i.e., with the process of real growth towards holiness. Condemned by Pope John Paul II (+2005) in the Apostolic Exhortation *Familiaris Consortio* (1981).[41]

Liberation Theology

Radical politicization of faith influential in Latin America, especially in the 1960s after the Council of Vatican II, where it became the political praxis of theologians such as Peruvian priest Gustavo Gutiérrez (b. 1928), Uruguayan Jesuit Juan Luis Segundo (+1996), and Spanish Jesuit Jon Sobrino (b. 1938) using "Marxist analysis." Judges ecclesial realities in light of the Marxist "class struggle," transforming even the "Eucharist" into a sacramental celebration of the "people's struggle." Transmutes Christianity into a purely temporal messianism, exchanging theological faith, hope, and charity for "fidelity to history," "confidence in the future," and "option for the poor." Participation in the class struggle is presented as a requirement of charity itself, with every affirmation of faith or theology subordinated to political criteria. Even the death of Christ is given an exclusively political interpretation. Its tenets were condemned in the 1984 *Instruction on Certain Aspects of the "Theology of Liberation"* from the Congregation for the Doctrine of the Faith.

[41] See 34.

Liturgical heresy (Anti-liturgical heresy)

General term coined by the French Benedictine Abbot Dom Prosper Guéranger (+1875) for certain doctrines and liturgical practices first introduced with Protestantism. They were later manifested in the Jansenist Synod of Pistoia (1786), promoted by certain deviations of the so-called "Liturgical Movement," and somewhat influential in the official liturgical reform following the Council of Vatican II. Its key elements include: contempt for tradition, fabrication of newly invented liturgical rites and formulas, abolition of actions and formulas of mystical signification, and a man-centered style of worship. Pope Pius XII (+1958) condemned several such tenets in the Encyclical *Mediator Dei* (1947), such as the altar in the shape of a table, turning towards the people, introducing vernacular language into the Eucharistic sacrifice, the separation of altar and tabernacle, and liturgical antiquarianism. His most significant condemnation referred to "the temerity and daring of those who introduce novel liturgical practices."[42]

Modernism

Maintains that Christian dogma is historically contingent, continuously evolving, ultimately inexpressible in rational formulae, and ultimately discernible only on a subjective basis. Pope Pius X (+1914) gave the most precise assessment of Modernism in affirming: "Were one to attempt the task of collecting together all the errors that have been broached against the faith and to concentrate the sap and substance of them all into one, he could not better succeed than the Modernists have done."[43]

---

[42] 59.
[43] See Encyclical *Pascendi Dominici Gregis* (September 8, 1907), 39.

MORAL RELATIVISM

Rejects all objective moral value, holding that moral good or evil is the determination of individuals, thus rendering the acknowledgment of truth ultimately impossible. Condemned by Pope John Paul II (+2005) in the Encyclical *Veritatis Splendor* (1993).

NEO-PAGANISM

Revival of ancient pagan religions, or the syncretistic adoption of tenets or expressions of the same; especially common in the practice of New Age, Yoga, Reiki, and other forms of Eastern mysticism.

NOUVELLE THEOLOGIE

French layman Maurice Blondel (+1949) formulated the philosophy on which the *nouvelle theologie* ("new theology") is based, whose main tenet is that theology, to remain alive, must move with the times and attribute to history an important place. This New Theology prefers to substitute for the clear metaphysical notions of St. Thomas Aquinas the fluid concepts of modern philosophies, to the harm of unchangeable Catholic doctrines. Main representatives included the French Jesuit Henri de Lubac (+1991) and the French Dominican Yves Congar (+1995). While the theologians of the movement generally preferred to call their movement *ressourcement* ("return to the sources") based on their return to original patristic thought, they nevertheless deviated in certain aspects from the longstanding theological tradition of the Catholic Church, thus creating a "new theology" that was to some extent a resurgent Modernism. Pope Pius XII (+1958) plainly condemned this new theological movement in the Encyclical *Humani generis* (1950), stating: "It is evident ... that such tentatives not only lead to what one calls dogmatic relativism, but that they actually contain it."[44]

Pentecostalism

Protestant system emphasizing the charismatic, demonstrative, sentimental, ecstatic, and irrational, with primacy on religious experience over doctrinal tenets.

Rahnerism

Named for German Jesuit priest Karl Rahner (+1984); a new concept of faith and theology with his "anthropological turn," which ultimately capitulates to enlightenment anthropocentrism and religious relativism, leading to a non-dogmatic and conceptually vague unity of all religions. Rahner propagated the theory of the "supernatural existential," holding that when a person accepts himself in his essential being, his existence is already supernatural — thus abolishing the difference between nature and the supernatural. This theory includes the notion of the "Anonymous Christian," hoping for universal salvation by stating that a person who professes disbelief can still live the requirements of the Christian faith and be saved. The Christian, therefore, coincides with the *human*, in that every man who accepts himself is a Christian, even if he does not know it. Rahnerism reduces Christianity to a purely conscious presentation of the human being in himself. It is a very grave doctrinal error because it declares personal justification as being already realized for every man without any participation of his will or free choice, with redemption guaranteed for all, as if sanctifying grace were ontologically present in each

[44] 16.

man simply because he is man. In 1962, Rahner's superiors informed him that he was under the pre-censorship of the Vatican, meaning that he could not publish or lecture without advance permission.

Religious Liberty

An imagined natural right, positively willed by God, inherent in every person, to unimpededly profess and propagate the religion of the choice of one's conscience (consequently even religious error) both individually and collectively; or the belief that States should or must recognize and protect the same by civil sanction, even despite the inherent psychological and moral degeneracy of certain religions (which is the case, e.g., with the Church of Satan, witchcraft, Wicca). Easily makes the individual conscience a source of rights and duties in religious matters, subordinating the objective to the subjective order. Such a notion of religious liberty has been rejected by the constant teaching of the Magisterium; e.g., by Pope Gregory XVI (+1846) in the Encyclical *Mirari vos* (1832), Pope Pius IX (+1878) in the *Syllabus Errorum* (1864),[45] Pope Leo XIII (+1903) in the Encyclicals *Immortale Dei* (1885) and *Libertas Praestantissimum* (1888), and Pope Pius XII (+1958) in his discourse *Ci riesce* (1953): "That which does not correspond to truth or to the norm of morality has objectively no right to exist, to be spread or to be activated."

Religious Pluralism

Indifferentist system holding all world religions as positively willed by God and sanctifying for their respective adherents.

[45] See I, 15–16.

Sedevacantism

From the Latin *sede vacante* ("the See is vacant"); notion that the Roman See has been vacant since the time of the popes of the Second Vatican Council.

Syncretism

General term for the fusion of (typically non-Christian) doctrinal or devotional elements, especially in acts of external religious observance.

21st CENTURY

Ecological Mysticism

Animist system that divinizes the natural world, personifying and idolizing it under ancient pagan titles (Pachamama, Gaia, etc.) or modern derivatives (Mother Earth, Mother Nature, etc.).

Gender ideology

Form of sexual ideology holding a dualistic anthropology; rejects the natural order of the two sexes, maintaining that one's inner self-experience constitutes the "gender" of the "true self" independent of the body. In its most radical form, *transgenderism* holds that one can "change" one's gender at will,to better conform with one's self-perception through chemicals, surgery, attire, or simple assertion. Such ideology was condemned by the Pontifical Council for the Family in *Family, Marriage and "De facto" Unions* (2000), and by the Congregation for the Doctrine of the Faith in *Letter to the*

Bishops of the Catholic Church on the Collaboration of Men and Women in the Church and in the World (2004).

HOMOSEXUAL IDEOLOGY

Rejects the mutual complementarity of male and female and/or the nature and purpose of the sexual faculties as manifested in the natural order created by God; maintains that God creates certain persons with unnatural sexual attractions as part of their innate identity, and/or that God wills such feelings to be acted upon. Used to justify sodomy, all kinds of same-sex eroticism, and especially its social or legal recognition as same-sex "registered partnerships," same-sex "civil unions," same-sex "stable couple unions," and "marriages" under the redefinition of the very nature of marriage as instituted by the Creator. Homosexual activity was more recently condemned by the Congregation for the Doctrine of the Faith in the Declaration *Persona humana* (1975) and by Pope John Paul II (+2005) in his Encyclical *Veritatis splendor* (1993),[46] and any form of same-sex "unions" were condemned by the Congregation for the Doctrine of the Faith in the document *Considerations Regarding Proposals to Give Legal Recognition to Unions Between Homosexual Persons* (2003).

MAGISTERIAL POSITIVISM

Holds that all teachings, acts, and commands of a pope or ecumenical council are automatically infallibly true, morally good, and necessary to obey. Implicitly gives primacy to the Magisterium above Holy Scripture and Tradition, as occurs when representatives of the Magisterium manifestly teach or act to undermine revealed truths or the perennial sacramental and liturgical praxis of the Church. Such was the case under Pope Paul VI (+1978), who sought in 1970 to proscribe the

---

[46] See 47.

venerable millennium-old Roman Rite of Mass and forbid its celebration, and with Pope Francis, who contradicted the Church's perennial moral and sacramental praxis in 2016 by authorizing the reception of Holy Communion by public adulterers,[47] and in 2023 by authorizing the blessing of adulterous or sodomitical couples.[48] Magisterial Positivism justifies all such deviations through an artificial "hermeneutic of continuity" or semantic exercises of "squaring the circle," or irrational obedience.

Transhumanism

Evolutionary concept of human nature, in which the final stage must be achieved by technological manipulation unto a certain self-perfection or alleged immortality. Pope Francis rejected transhumanism in 2016 as "the annihilation of man as the image of God."[49]

---

[47] See Letter to the Bishops of the Buenos Aires region of September 5, 2016. In his later audience with the Cardinal Secretary of State, "Ex audientia SS.mi" (June 5, 2017), the pope declared this approval to be "authentic Magisterium."

[48] See Declaration *Fiducia Supplicans* on the Pastoral Meaning of Blessings from December 18, 2023.

[49] Dialogue with the Bishops of Poland in Krakow, August 2, 2016.

Part III

Topical Discussion of Errors

Errors about God and the Trinity

What is the principal source of all errors about God and divine revelation?

Sin. Pride and lust darken the mind and especially lead man to prefer his own judgment and personal comfort over submission to a divinely revealed body of doctrine, morals, and worship.

What are the major errors about God and revelation today?

Regarding His existence: atheism and agnosticism. Regarding His communication with us: naturalism, deism, and modernism.

What should we think of atheist professionals in the natural sciences who claim to disprove the existence of God?

They have exceeded the inherent limits of all natural science and have adopted the errors of a faulty philosophy. They are to be pitied, and it is necessary to pray for them, so that they can discover the truth by God's grace, the teaching of the Church, and the witness of the faithful.

How can we defend the existence of God, if evil exists in the world?

It is impossible for God, Who is all good, wise, and powerful, to be the author of evil. Rather, suffering, sickness, and death are the consequence of our first parents' rebellion against God. Evil therefore comes from the free choice of His creatures and the resulting imperfections in creation, which He merely permits.

What are the principal religious errors regarding the Holy Trinity?

Arianism and *Macedonianism,* fourth-century heresies restricting true divinity to the Father and denying the eternal divinity of the Son and Holy Spirit; 2. *Islam, contemporary Judaism,* various *Unitarian* sects, and *Modernism* within the Catholic Church, all of which reject God's self-revelation as a Trinity of divine and consubstantial Persons; 3. *Buddhism, Hinduism, pantheism,* and other systems that reject the simplicity or unity of God independent of creatures.

Errors about the Creation

What of theories claiming that the universe began spontaneously, either by itself or from some preexisting matter?

These are errors of philosophy rather than claims of empirical science, and are also impossibilities. Nothing can come from nothing, and nothing can cause itself to exist.

Hasn't the Genesis account of Creation been disproven by the natural sciences?

No. On the contrary, the ongoing discoveries of sedimentology, astrophysics, microbiology, genetics, and other disciplines continue to confirm the sacred history of Genesis in those truths that, according to the Magisterium, this history is meant to teach us.[50]

Then creation is really distinct from God, and subordinated to Him?

Yes. Throughout history, various false religions and pantheistic philosophies have regarded creation as a divine manifestation, emanation, or somehow part of God (see Rom 1; and Ws 13) — but the true God is in no way dependent on creatures.

In our time, what is the chief error about this distinction between God and creation?

The personification and even deification of nature, often manifested in forms of environmental idolatry, ecological mysticism, Earth-goddess rituals, animism, and other forms of pagan worship.

What is the error of so-called "transhumanism"?

Man's attempt to negate his creatureliness and elevate himself to a higher level of existence by manipulating human nature through technology (genetic engineering, cryonics, implants with

---

[50] Regarding the truth of this sacred history, see Pontifical Biblical Commission, *Concerning the Historical Character of the First Three Chapters of Genesis* (June 30, 1909). See also Pope Pius XII, Encyclicals *Humani Generis* (August 12, 1950), 22, and *Divino Afflante Spiritu* (September 30, 1943), 1; Pope Leo XIII, *Providentissimus Deus* (November 18, 1893), 21; Pope Pius X, Encyclical *Lamentabili Sane* (July 3, 1907), 11; and Pope Benedict XV, *Spiritus Paraclitus* (September 15, 1920), 19.

brain-computer interfaces, etc.), in order to achieve self-perfection or even an alleged immortality. Transhumanism embodies man's original sin of wanting to be like God without grace.

Is man a creature that the Creator has willed for its own sake?[51]

No. Although man should never be used as a mere means to an end, the notion that man exists simply "for his own sake" is the self-referential error of *anthropocentrism*, rooted in the un-Christian philosophy of Immanuel Kant (1724–1804). Rather, "God wills things apart from Himself insofar as they are ordered to His own goodness as their end";[52] and, "God is the only end of man."[53]

Are Satan and the other demons merely figurative representations of evil in the Bible?

No. We know by revelation and reason that they are real and personal beings of pure spirit, invisible, unchangeably malicious, and constantly active in our fallen world.

Can the demons ever repent and convert back to God?

No. As purely spiritual beings, they foresaw all the consequences of their choice and fixed their wills in evil forever.

---

[51] The Council of Vatican II's document *Gaudium et Spes* made the ambiguous affirmation that "man is the only creature on earth that God has willed for its own sake" (24).
[52] ST I, q. 19, a. 3, c.
[53] Pope Leo XIII, Encyclical *Tametsi Futura Prospicientibus* (November 1, 1900), 6.

What is the final aim of Satan's seduction of men?

He aims that men adore him instead of God: "The devil, as he is the apostate angel, can only go to… deceive and lead astray the mind of man into disobeying the commandments of God, and gradually to darken the hearts of those who would endeavor to serve Him, to the forgetting of the true God, and to the adoration of himself as God."[54]

Why is so-called "feminism" an ideology to be on guard against?

Under the praiseworthy guise of advocating for the civil rights of women, feminism has tended to destroy all that is truly feminine, by undermining sociocultural norms based on the natural distinction between the sexes. In the name of "sameness," sexual complementarity is lost, and the irreplaceable role of women and mothers is abandoned in marriage, family, and broader society.

Who denies the spirituality of the soul?

Chiefly *materialists*, who imagine that nothing exists in the universe but matter. In addition to contradicting the very idea of knowledge, this notion inevitably gives rise to the eugenical mindset, which seeks the material control of human procreation and the tyrannical rule of the strong over the weak, as the history of the last century attests.

Who denies human freedom?

Chiefly *determinists*, who hold that human acts are determined by preexisting causes — e.g., social circumstances or other impersonal forces (fate, stars, etc.) — and that men are therefore not to be held responsible for their own actions.

---

[54] St. Irenaeus, *Adversus Haereses*, bk. 5, chap. 24, no. 3.

Who denies the immortality of the soul?

Chiefly *atheists, materialists,* and others who imagine that they are nothing but well-adapted animals; while others claim that God annihilates the human soul after death, which is likewise a grave error.[55]

Who denies the fundamental unity of body and soul in man?

Chiefly the ancient *Gnostics,* as well as various dualistic and neo-Gnostic ideologies of our time, e.g., *transgenderism* and *transhumanism.* All of these errors view man's body as some kind of cage or machine, a manipulable and dispensable apparatus, controlled by some inner essence or so-called "true self."

Who denies that the body of man was created by God?

Chiefly Darwinists and other atheists, who claim that man's body was formed over countless ages of random and gradual development from some ancient protoplasm, in a process generally called human evolution.

Why is great caution required in considering evolutionary theories?

Because such theories have yet to be scientifically proven, have no evident basis in Scripture or Tradition, and are remarkably similar to ancient Gnostic myths.[56]

---

[55] See Pope Leo X, Bull *Apostolici Regiminis* (December 19, 1513).

[56] Second-century Gnostics taught that man was formed in an imperfect state by seven preternatural archons, "yet was unable to stand erect ... but wriggled on the ground like a worm. Then the power above taking pity upon him, since he was made after his likeness, sent forth a spark of life, which gave man an erect posture, compacted his joints, and made him live" (St. Irenaeus, *Adv. Haer.*, bk. 1, chap. 24).

Has the Church definitively rejected the evolutionary theory of polygenism, the notion that men today evolved from two or more distinct ancestral types?

Yes. "The faithful cannot embrace that opinion which maintains that either after Adam there existed on this earth true men who did not take their origin through natural generation from him as from the first parent of all, or that 'Adam' represents a certain number of first parents. Now it is in no way apparent how such an opinion can be reconciled with that which the sources of revealed truth and the documents of the teaching authority of the Church propose with regard to original sin, which proceeds from a sin actually committed by an individual Adam and which, through generation, is passed on to all and is in everyone as his own."[57]

Is every human person created as a man or woman, male or female?

Yes. The male and female sexes are fundamental and unalterable biological realities, and the body of each person reveals whether they are a man or a woman. "Male and female [God] created them" (Gn 1:27), and "He who made man from the beginning, made them male and female" (Mt 19:4*).

What of the novel claim that our "gender" may not correspond to our biological sex?

This error of *gender ideology* or *gender theory* denies the reality of the two sexes and replaces it with unlimited private choice, claiming that one's inner thoughts and feelings or merely social and

---

[57] Pope Pius XII, *Humani Generis*, 37.

educational conditioning constitute the "gender" of the "true self"—a kind of Gnostic and ultimately Satanic dualism that must be rejected.

What of the claim that our "sexual orientation" may not correspond to our biological sex?

The notion that God creates a disordered sexual attraction in some persons, or that He wills such feelings to be acted upon in some cases, is contrary to both reason and revelation, "for God is not a God of disorder, but of peace" (1 Cor 14:33*).

What are the main errors about the last things in our own time?

1. The refusal to acknowledge any life after death, as in atheism or materialism; 2. The rejection of the doctrine of purgatory, as in Protestantism; 3. The denial of an objective moral law with eternal reward for good and evil, as in relativism; 4. The claim that wicked souls are destroyed after death, as in annihilationism; 5. The claim that all men will ultimately be saved and attain heaven independently of their deeds, as in universalism; 6. The claim that the human soul begins a new life in a different physical form or body after death, as in the notions of reincarnation, rebirth, or transmigration; 7. The claim that hell may be empty of human souls, as in the theory of Hans Urs von Balthasar; 8. The claim that in the end of time all men and even Satan and the demons will be saved, as in the heresy of *apokatastasis*.

Errors about the Incarnation

What is natural religion?

The sum of those truths and precepts concerning man's relations with God, which human reason is capable of achieving on its own; e.g., the existence of God, His providence, the obligation of worshipping Him, etc.

Is natural religion sufficient for man?

No. Since God has revealed Himself to man, all are obliged to seek and submit to this divine revelation, i.e., to profess supernatural religion.

What is supernatural religion?

The sum of those truths which God Himself has revealed, and the positive commands which He has made; e.g., the mysteries of the Incarnation and the Redemption, the proper worship that He desires, etc.

Was the religion that God gave to man at the beginning complete and final?

No. This religion was developed by degrees over time, passing through three historical phases: 1. *Patriarchal* religion (especially in Abel the Just and Abraham[58]); 2. *Mosaic* religion; and finally, 3. *Christian* religion. The first extends from the Fall of man to

---

[58] See St. Augustine, *Serm.* 341, chap. 9, no. 11; *De Civitate Dei*, bk. 18, chap. 51. Abraham saw the day of Christ and was glad, see Jn 8:56.

Moses; the second, from the Mosaic Law to Jesus Christ; the third will endure without change until the end of time.

Are these phases to be regarded as three different religions?

No. There has only ever been one true religion, successively developed and perfected over time, until its definitive establishment in the Person and mission of Jesus Christ.

Why is Jesus Christ the central figure in the divine plan?

Because: 1. By Him all things were made and continue in existence; 2. He is the head of the Church, which will continue to the end of time; 3. He is the source of all grace; 4. He is the goal of all creation as the infinite and complete good.

Is Christ merely a "privileged way" to God, among many other possible ways?

No. Such a notion expresses *religious indifferentism*, the belief that all religions are channels of grace, holiness, and salvation, even if some are more "efficacious" than others. This rejects the unity of the divine plan, insults our Redeemer, and contradicts His most solemn words: "No man comes to the Father except through Me" (Jn 14:6*), "I am the way" (see Jn 14:6), and "there is no other name given under heaven whereby we must be saved" (Acts 4:12*).

What does religious indifferentism lead to?

1. *Relativism*, which makes each community or individual the sole determiner of truth and falsity, good and evil; 2. *Agnosticism*, which views God's existence, knowability, or salvific work as uncertain;

3. *Atheism*, which finally denies God's existence altogether. Religious indifferentism has therefore been strongly censured by the Church.[59]

What were the main heresies about the Incarnation in the early centuries?

Those of: 1. *Adoptionists* and *Arians*, who denied the eternal divine nature and personhood of Jesus Christ; 2. *Gnostics* and *Docetists*, who denied that He had a human body; 3. *Apollinarists*, who denied that He had a human soul; 4. *Nestorians*, who claimed there are two persons in Jesus Christ; 5. *Monophysites*, who claimed that His human nature was absorbed by the divine nature; 6. *Monothelites*, who denied that He had a human will.

Of these errors, are any still to be found today?

Yes. Chief among them is always Arianism, because many acknowledge Jesus as a great moral teacher or spiritual leader, but reject Him as their "Lord and God" (see Jn 20:28). Every departure from Catholic doctrine is essentially an error about the Incarnation.

Why is it necessary to believe and profess the Incarnation of the Son of God?

All life and existence hinges on the Incarnation of the Son of God. Those who deny it will have sorrow in this life, and be eternally lost in the next: "If you believe not that I am He, you shall die in your sin" (Jn 8:24*).

---

[59] See especially Pope Pius IX, *Syllabus Errorum* (December 8, 1864), in the Appendix below.

Errors about the Redemption

What are the main errors about the Redemption?

The appearance of Protestantism in the sixteenth century, having fractured into thousands of different sects since then, was founded on a false notion of the Redemption and the application of its fruits — i.e., *justification* — apart from our active cooperation with grace.

Of these errors, are any of them especially common today?

Yes, these three grave errors: 1. Man can be saved apart from faith in Jesus Christ; 2. Faith in Jesus alone is sufficient for salvation, such that man is not also obliged to observe the commandments of God and His Church; 3. Man is unable to fulfill these commandments, such that God demands the impossible.[60]

What do these errors have in common?

Each may imply an acknowledgment of Christ as Redeemer, but refuses to adore and obey Him as King and Lawgiver. Christ is either the Lord of all, or He is not the Lord at all.

What ancient heresy denied that Christ truly died on the Cross?

Docetism, which maintained that the body of Jesus was merely a phantom or illusion, and that the Son of God did not truly die on a Cross for our redemption.

---

[60] These and many similar errors are condemned in the Council of Trent's famous *Decree on Justification* (Session 6 [January 13, 1547]).

Why did Our Lord permit His body to be buried?

To affirm the reality of His death, render His Resurrection more glorious, fulfill numerous prophecies, and stand as a mystical symbol: as the body of Adam was drawn from the virgin earth by divine power, so Christ would rise from a virgin tomb by His own divine power, showing Himself able to raise all men from their graves at the end of time.

Why has God given such striking proofs of Christ's Resurrection?

Because this mystery is the very foundation of Christianity. If Christ has not risen, His religion is an imposture. If He has risen, then He is God, His religion is divine, and all must profess it. "If Christ has not been raised, then our proclamation has been in vain and your faith has been in vain. We are even found to be misrepresenting God, because we testified of God that He raised Christ—whom He did not raise if it is true that the dead are not raised.... If Christ has not been raised, your faith is futile and you are still in your sins.... If for this life only we have hoped in Christ, we are of all people most to be pitied" (1 Cor 15:14–15, 17, 19).

Will all men ultimately go to heaven?

No. Only those who receive the fruits of this Redemption will attain heaven. God will not save free creatures without their cooperation or against their will: "God created us without us, but He did not will to save us without us."[61]

---

[61] St. Augustine, *Serm.* 169.

Is it reasonable to hope, as in the theory of *apokatastasis* or of Hans Urs von Balthasar, that all men will go to heaven?

No. The Son of God has warned us most solemnly: "The gate is narrow and the road is hard that leads to life, and there are few who find it" (Mt 7:14).

Can the saving power of Christ's Redemption be mediated through any religion?

No. It is a condemned error to hold that "man may, in the observance of any religion whatever, find the way of eternal salvation, and arrive at eternal salvation."[62]

Do Our Lord's merits dispense us from acquiring any merit ourselves?

No. We must also strive to cooperate with grace and merit heaven by our good works: "With fear and trembling work out your salvation" (Phil 2:12*). Of themselves, our good works have no value—but through the merits of Jesus Christ, they are worthy of the reward of grace.

Is it really possible for man to reject God, and turn away from Him forever?

Yes. God respects those who have freely chosen the obstinate rejection of Him, and does not force them to be with Him for all eternity. *Hell* is the name for that place and condition in which those who reject God are condemned to suffer eternally away from His presence, with the demons.

---

[62] Pope Pius IX, *Syllabus Errorum*, III, 16.

Has the Church's Magisterium infallibly defined hell as being eternal?

Yes. "If anyone says or holds that the punishment of demons and impious human beings is temporary and that it will have an end at some time, and that there will be a restoration of demons and impious human beings, let him be anathema."[63]

ERRORS ABOUT THE CHURCH

Are all religions, with their respective forms of worship, equally pleasing to God?

No. Only the religion established by God and fulfilled in Christ, with its divinely revealed worship, is supernatural, holy, and pleasing to God. All other religions are inherently false, and their forms of worship pernicious, or at least unavailing for eternal life.

Why are non-Christian religions inherently false?

"There can be no true religion other than that which is founded on the revealed word of God: which revelation, begun from the beginning and continued under the Old Law, Christ Jesus Himself perfected under the New Law."[64]

Why are non-Christian forms of worship pernicious, or at least unavailing to salvation?

God has revealed the way in which He desires to be worshipped in Christ, and "the Catholic Church is alone in keeping the true

---

[63] Pope Vigilius, *Anathematismi contra Originem* (in 543), can. 9.
[64] Pope Pius XI, Encyclical *Mortalium Animos* (January 6, 1928), 6.

worship."[65] To practice a false worship, or neglect to discover and offer right worship, offends God and harms the soul.

Is Judaism a source of sanctifying grace and salvation for its adherents?

No. Even in the time before Christ, no one was saved by works of the Old Law, but only by faith in the coming Redeemer. This Law, with its precepts and ceremonies, was fulfilled and surpassed by the New Covenant in Jesus Christ (see Rom 3:28; Gal 2:16).

What of John 4:22, where Our Lord says: "Salvation is from the Jews"?

Jesus Christ is Himself the fulfillment of this prophecy, whereas contemporary Judaism, also called Talmudic or Rabbinic Judaism — without temple, priesthood, or sacrifice — is not the same religion that God established in the Old Testament. Rejecting the true Messiah, the Old Law has thus become "both dead and deadly."[66]

Who are the true children of Abraham?

Not those who boast of genealogical descent from Abraham, but only those holding the faith of Abraham, with belief in the coming Christ (see Jn 8:56). St. Paul states unequivocally: "If you belong to Christ, then you are Abraham's offspring, heirs according to the promise" (Gal 3:29).

---

[65] Pope Pius XI, *Mortalium Animos*, 11.
[66] ST I-II, q. 103, a. 4, rep. 1.

Is explicit faith in Jesus Christ necessary for contemporary Jews to be saved?

Yes, the same as with all men. Those who willfully reject Jesus Christ as the Savior are excluded from salvation, "cut off," as St. Paul teaches: "See then the goodness and the severity of God: towards them indeed that are fallen [Jews], the severity; but towards thee, the goodness of God, if thou abide in goodness, otherwise thou also shalt be cut off. And they also, if they abide not still in unbelief, shall be grafted in: for God is able to graft them in again" (Rom 11:22–23).

What of Romans 11:29: "The gifts and the calling of God are irrevocable"?

Saint Paul speaks here of God's abiding love for the Jews, foretelling their conversion to Christ before the end of time. Until then, contemporary Judaism as a whole exists as a rejection of God's calling, since there can be no fidelity to the Old Covenant where its fulfillment in the New is denied: "If you believed Moses, you would believe Me, for he wrote of Me" (Jn 5:46). The call of God is to believe in His Son, and those who believe are sons of Abraham, heirs of the promise (see Gal 3:29).

Then God does not will the diversity of religions found in the world today?[67]

No, He does not. God cannot be the author of religious error or any other evil, because "God is true" (Jn 3:33). "It is necessarily impossible for God, the Supreme Truth, to be the author of any

---

[67] As affirmed by Pope Francis together with Sheikh Ahmed Al-Tayeb, Grand Imam of Al-Azhar, in *A Document on Human Fraternity for World Peace and Living Together* (February 4, 2019).

error whatsoever."[68] Rather, false religions arise from the deception of the devil, sin, and ignorance—evils that God merely tolerates in our fallen world.

Do Muslims adore the one and merciful God "together with us" Catholics?[69]

No. Catholics consciously profess and adore "one God in Trinity, and Trinity in Unity,"[70] not simply "the one God"; whereas one of the most famous and frequent Muslim prayers, the Al-Ikhlas Ayat, solemnly rejects this divine revelation, in saying: "He is Allah, the one and only; Allah, the eternal, absolute; he begets not, nor is he begotten; and there is none like unto him."[71]

Is it true to say that Muslims hold the faith of Abraham?[72]

No. Abraham saw three and adored one[73] (see Gn 18:2–3) and rejoiced in the vision of the future Redeemer (see Jn 8:56), excluding neither Christ nor the Trinity in his faith. Conversely, the Muslim explicitly excludes faith in Christ and the Holy Trinity.

---

[68] Pope Leo XIII, *Providentissimus Deus*, 20.
[69] For this ambiguous affirmation, see Council of Vatican II, *Lumen Gentium*, 16.
[70] Athanasian Creed, *Quicumque Vult*.
[71] Known as the Declaration of God's Unity and Al-Tawhid (monotheism), this prayer of Surah 112 is counted among the most important chapters of the Quran and considered by Muslims worldwide to be equal in value to one-third of the entire Quran.
[72] See this misleading phrase in Council of Vatican II, *Lumen Gentium*, 16, and repeated in *Catechism of the Catholic Church*, 841.
[73] Pope St. Gregory the Great says: "Abraham saw the day of the Lord when he received at his home the three angels of the most Holy Trinity: three guests whom he assuredly addressed as one, for even though the Persons of the Trinity are three in number, the nature of the deity is one" (*In Ev.*, Hom. 18, no. 3).

Does the Muslim religion condemn those who profess the divinity of Jesus Christ and adore Him?

Yes. The Quran, its central religious text, teaches: "The Christians say, 'The Messiah is the son of Allah.' That is their statement from their mouths; they imitate the saying of those who disbelieved [before them]. May Allah destroy them."[74] And: "Fight those People of the Book who do not believe in Allah, nor in the Last Day, and do not take as unlawful what Allah and his Messenger have declared as unlawful, and do not profess the faith of truth; (fight them) until they pay *jizyah* [a tax] with their own hands while they are subdued."[75]

Does Our Lord Jesus Christ warn those who pretend to adore only the one and merciful God, or only the Father, while refusing to adore Him, the Son of God?

Yes. "Whoever believes in the Son has eternal life; whoever disobeys the Son will not see life, but must endure God's wrath" (Jn 3:36). "All may honor the Son just as they honor the Father. Anyone who does not honor the Son does not honor the Father who sent Him" (Jn 5:23).

Does the Holy Spirit use false religions to impart grace and salvation to man?[76]

No. Although God is able to give graces to a man who practices a false religion in view of his innocent ignorance and sincere good

---

[74] The Quran, Surah 9:30.
[75] The Quran, Surah 9:29.
[76] For this confusing assertion, see Council of Vatican II, Decree *Unitatis Redintegratio* (November 21, 1964), 3; restated in *Catechism of the Catholic Church*, 819.

will, such graces would in nowise be *mediated by* or *owing to* the false religion itself. Rather, grace may be given despite the man's error, and in order to lead him out of that error into the truth of right faith.[77]

Is it necessary to belong to the Catholic Church to be saved?

Yes. This is the meaning of the affirmation often repeated by the Church Fathers, popes, and councils: *extra Ecclesiam nulla salus*, "outside the Church there is no salvation."[78] "The Church, now sojourning on earth as an exile, is necessary for salvation.... Whosoever, therefore, knowing that the Catholic Church was made necessary by Christ, would refuse to enter or to remain in it, could not be saved."[79]

Doesn't God want all men to be saved?

Yes. As a loving Father, God "desires everyone to be saved and to come to the knowledge of the truth" (1 Tm 2:4). This is why He established His Church as the ordinary and universal means of salvation. "He cannot have God for his Father, who does not have the Church for his mother."[80]

---

[77] As with the case of the Ethiopian eunuch in Acts 8:26–40.
[78] St. Cyprian, *Ep.* 73, no. 21; see St. Cyprian, *De unit.*, no. 6, 13; St. Fulgentius of Ruspe, *De Fide*, 37, 34; Council of Lateran IV, "Profession of Faith" (November 30, 1215); Pope Eugene IV, *Cantate Domino*; Pope Pius XII, *Mystici Corporis Christi*, 3.
[79] Council of Vatican II, *Lumen Gentium*, 14; Decree *Ad Gentes* (December 7, 1965), 7.
[80] St. Cyprian of Carthage, *De unit.*, no. 6.

What about the many non-Catholic groups claiming the title of "Christian" or "Church"?

Those that hold Jesus as Lord but do not profess the entirety of His doctrine or participate in the unity of His Church have no proper claim to such titles. While often composed of men of good will, these communities are separated from the true Church as products typically of *heresies* or *schisms*.

Are these groups simply branches, extensions, or partial sharings in the one true Church?

No. "Jesus Christ did not, in point of fact, institute a Church to embrace several communities similar in nature, but in themselves distinct, and lacking those bonds which render the Church unique and indivisible."[81] Christ founded only one true Church: the Catholic Church. Established upon St. Peter, whose See was in Rome and whose successors still reign there, it is also called the Roman Catholic Church.

How may the one true Church be identified?

It may be known especially by those four *marks* or distinctive notes that Christ gave to it, which we profess in the Niceno-Constantinopolitan Creed: the Church is "one, holy, catholic, and apostolic."

Must the true Church exist with all of these marks in an indestructible totality?

Yes. 1. If the Church were not *one*, it would not be true, for unity is an essential aspect of truth; 2. If the Church were not *holy*, it

---

[81] Pope Leo XIII, Encyclical *Satis Cognitum* (June 29, 1896), 4.

could not sanctify souls; 3. If the Church were not *catholic*, it could not offer salvation to all people in all times and places; 4. If the Church were not *apostolic*, it would not have its doctrine, mission, and authority from Christ, but would instead be a merely human institution.

What is the mission of the Church on earth?

The Catholic Church alone bears the divine authority and mandate to teach, govern, and sanctify all men in Jesus Christ until He returns in glory.

Are there widespread errors about the mission of the Church today?

Yes. Many mistakenly believe the Church's mission to be one of improving the temporal welfare of man, as if the Son of God became incarnate to establish a humanitarian service organization for combatting poverty, disease, or environmental pollution. Others mistakenly look for a "new humanity" in which "a real and lasting peace will only be possible on the basis of a global ethic of solidarity and ... shared responsibility in the whole human family," where the Church merely "works for the advancement of humanity and of universal fraternity."[82]

Who are not members of the Catholic Church?

All the non-baptized, including Jews, Muslims, and pagans.

---

[82] For this nebulous assertion, see Pope Francis, Encyclical *Fratelli Tutti* (October 3, 2020), 127, 276.

Who else does not belong to the unity of the Catholic Church?

All the baptized whose crimes and sins have impeded the efficacy of their baptismal character, separating them from the spiritual goods of the Church. These include heretics, schismatics, excommunicates, and apostates.

Who are pagans?

Those who have never accepted the Christian Faith or received sacramental baptism, although they may belong to some other organized religion (e.g., Buddhists, Hindus).

Who are heretics?

Those who have received baptism, yet obstinately deny some article of Faith which must be held (e.g., Protestants, Modernists).

Who are schismatics?

Those who received baptism, yet have been separated from the unity of the Catholic Church by refusing to recognize the Supreme Pontiff or have canonical communion with him and the other members of the Church (e.g., the Orthodox).

Are so-called "sedevacantists" in schism?

Yes, inasmuch as one who obstinately refuses to recognize a lawfully reigning pope is by that fact a schismatic.

Is any act of disobedience to a command of the pope by itself schismatic?

No. One is not schismatic if he resists a pope or refuses to obey a particular teaching or command of his that is manifestly contrary to natural or divine law, or that would harm or undermine the integrity of the Catholic Faith or the sacredness of the liturgy. In such cases, disobedience and resistance to the pope is permissible and sometimes obligatory.[83]

Who are excommunicates?

Catholics who, for some grave crime, have been cut off from the visible communion of the Church and deprived of its spiritual blessings. As in the case of St. Joan of Arc, the legal penalty of excommunication may be levied unjustly, and so be without judicial standing or effect.

Who are apostates?

Those who, after having professed the Catholic Faith, have now totally repudiated it.

Who err regarding the visibility of the Church?

Those who believe that the Church is merely an invisible association of men united by shared beliefs and interior dispositions, as is commonly held among Protestants.

---

[83] In 357, St. Athanasius refused to obey Pope Liberius, who commanded him to recognize the Arian bishops of the Orient. Thereupon Pope Liberius excommunicated St. Athanasius.

Who err regarding the perpetuity of the Church?

Those who believe that the true Church once ceased to exist or was essentially corrupted, as held by Mormons; or that it could give way to some new form in the future, as held by Modernists.

Who err regarding the indefectibility of the Church?

Those who believe that the constant Magisterium of the Church has or could definitively promulgate false doctrines, command heretical worship, or give false sacraments, contrary to the promise of her divine Founder that the gates of hell will not prevail against it (see Mt 16:18).

Who err regarding the infallibility of the Church?

Those who believe that the Church can definitively and formally hold or teach doctrinal error, or that past definitive teaching may be superseded in a process of doctrinal evolution, or who construe the charism of infallibility too broadly, as if individual members of the Church were entirely incapable of error.

Why is it dangerous to misconstrue the Church's infallibility too broadly?

Because one risks being scandalized by heretical clergy, and it is a painful fact that the most pernicious errors in history have sprung from the ranks of the ordained. Christ warns us to beware of such ravening wolves and false shepherds (see Mt 7:15; 23:13; 18:6; and Acts 20:29).

Why is the Catholic Church holy?

Because: 1. Its founder is the Son of God; 2. It is animated by the Holy Spirit; 3. Its dogmas, morals, worship, and discipline withdraw man from evil and lead to virtue; 4. All who have kept her commands have been good and virtuous, and all who have followed her counsels perfectly have become great saints; 5. Innumerable miracles have occurred in her fold.

Then why are scandalous sinners sometimes found within the Church?

The Church is holy, "though she has sinners in her bosom, because she herself has no other life but that of grace: it is by living by her life that her members are sanctified; it is by removing themselves from her life that they fall into sins and disorders that prevent the radiation of her sanctity."[84]

Why does God permit scandals in His Church?

In His mysterious providence, God permits the scandal of evildoers in His Church, as part of His design to sanctify and perfect the living members of the Church in every age. "For it must needs be that scandals come: but nevertheless woe to that man by whom the scandal comes" (Mt 18:7*). "Indeed, there have to be factions among you, for only so will it become clear who among you are genuine" (1 Cor 11:19).

---

[84] Pope Paul VI, Motu Proprio *Solemni Hac Liturgia* (June 30, 1968).

Authority in the Church

Who may authoritatively interpret both Scripture and Tradition?

Only the infallible teaching authority of the Magisterium, the formal teaching office of the Catholic Church, which is exercised by the pope alone or by the pope together with the bishops.

Is the Magisterium also a source of divine revelation?

No. The Magisterium is only the servant, guardian, and expositor of God's revelation: "Not so that they might make known some new doctrine, but that, by [God's] assistance, they might religiously guard and faithfully expound the revelation or Deposit of Faith transmitted by the apostles."[85]

Can the Magisterium change the content of this Deposit of Faith?

No. "Heaven and earth shall pass away, but My words shall never pass away" (Mt 24:35*). It is beyond the power of the Church to add to, subtract from, or alter the content of divine revelation, for she is charged strictly to teach "all those things whatsoever I have commanded you" (Mt 28:20*).

What is the true meaning of the expression living Magisterium?

It means that the apostolic preaching, voiced through the Church's Magisterium, will not cease until the end of the world. The voice

---

[85] Council of Vatican I, Dogmatic Constitution *Pastor Aeternus* (July 18, 1870).

of the apostles still lives and speaks when their successors, in an unbroken and faithful tradition, preserve and transmit the revealed truths; passing the living torch of the immutable doctrine of Faith, always *eodem dogmate, eodem sensu, eademque sententia*—"the same dogma, in the same sense, and in the same meaning."[86]

What of a development of doctrine, subject to changing circumstances?

The expressions "living tradition," "living Magisterium," "hermeneutic of continuity," and "development of doctrine," properly understood, can only mean that a greater clarity or precision is given to the same changeless content of divine revelation over time. Such new insights can never contradict what the Church has previously and definitively proposed, because Christ promised that the Holy Spirit would not reveal anything new, but only remind the disciples of what He told them (see Jn 14:26).

What authority has Christ given to the teaching Church?

He has invested the Church with His own triple authority in teaching, sanctifying, and governing. The pastors of His Church must therefore *instruct* the faithful in right doctrine, *sanctify* them by properly administering the sacraments and dispensing blessings, and *direct* them by good laws fostering upright moral lives.

To whom does this authority in the Church belong?

It belongs to the pope principally and universally, and to the other bishops within their dioceses. It is to these alone, in the person of

---

[86] Council of Vatican I, *Dei Filius*.

St. Peter and the other apostles, that Christ said: "Go therefore and make disciples of all nations" (Mt 28:19).

What are the most common errors about authority in the Church?

1. Various forms of *conciliarism*, limiting papal authority by the authority of bishops gathered in council; 2. *Gallicanism* or *Statism*, subjecting the authority of pope and bishops to the civil power; 3. *Magisterial positivism*, receiving every word of a living pope or bishop as inherently true, good, infallible, and necessary to obey; 4. *Protestantism*, viewing private judgment as an infallible authority in matters of faith and morals.

Can non-infallible and non-definitive teachings or commands of a pope or council be later reformulated for greater clarity, or even corrected?

Yes. Such teachings can be reformed later by an infallible act of the Magisterium. Commands issued on a prudential level — as the Fourth Lateran Council's recommendation of a Crusade, or the command that Jews in Catholic territories wear distinctive clothing — may be corrected by a change of laws, or by the refusal to implement such measures. Such reformable acts are especially noticeable among affirmations of the Second Vatican Council that are in themselves ambiguous and can lead to an erroneous understanding.[87]

---

[87] E.g., the assertion in *Lumen Gentium* 16 that says Muslims adore "together with us" Catholics the one God; or the assertion in *Dignitatis Humanae* 2 that says that the human person has a natural right to spread the religion of his choice (even if it were a false religion) without being impeded by civil law.

Then a pope is not infallible in all that he teaches or commands at every moment?

No. A pope is guaranteed to be free from all possibility of error only when he restates prior infallible teaching, or makes an *ex cathedra* pronouncement—a teaching that: 1. Concerns a matter of faith or morals; 2. Is addressed to the universal Church; 3. Is proposed in virtue of the pope's supreme apostolic office; 4. Is formulated as a final and binding definition.

Which heresies deny the pope's full and immediate power of teaching and government in the universal Church?

Conciliarism maintained that an ecumenical council is above the pope.[88] Similar heresies include the Orthodox Church's concept of synodality (*sobornost* in Russian), as well as episcopalism and Gallicanism, all of which claim that the college of bishops has universal jurisdiction and teaching power over the Church, with the pope being only "first among equals."

Has the Church infallibly condemned the substantial error of these theories?

Yes. "If anyone says that the Roman Pontiff has merely an office of supervision and guidance, and not the full and supreme power of jurisdiction over the whole Church, and this not only in matters of faith and morals, but also in those which concern the discipline and government of the Church dispersed throughout the whole world; or that he has only the principal part, but not the absolute

---

[88] A heresy propagated partly by the Council of Constance (1414–1418) and by the schismatic part of the Council of Basel (1431–1449), first explicitly condemned by Pope Pius II in 1460 with the Bull *Exsecrabilis*.

fullness, of this supreme power; or that this power of his is not ordinary and immediate both over all and each of the churches and over all and each of the pastors and faithful: let him be anathema."[89]

Is a particular council or synod infallible in its teaching?

No. However, its decrees could be made universally binding by the express declaration of the pope.

Are the teachings of an ecumenical council infallible?

Like the Supreme Pontiff's *ex cathedra* statements, an ecumenical council is infallible in its approved and solemn dogmatic definitions. Its other statements, disciplinary norms, pastoral provisions, etc. are beyond the scope of infallibility, and subject to possible future revision.

Why is Vatican II the clearest example of an ecumenical council emitting non-infallible teachings?

Because it was not convoked to infallibly pronounce new dogmas or propose definitive teachings, but to offer a pastoral explanation of the truths of the Faith, as asserted by Pope John XXIII: "[This Council's] magisterium is predominantly pastoral in character,"[90] and "the salient point of this Council is not a discussion of one article or another of the fundamental doctrine of the Church."[91] Pope Paul VI was also very clear in stating: "Given the Council's pastoral character, it avoided pronouncing, in an extraordinary manner, dogmas endowed with the note of infallibility."[92]

---

[89] Council of Vatican I, *Pastor Aeternus*.
[90] Opening Speech to the Council (October 11, 1962).
[91] Opening Speech (October 11, 1962).
[92] *General Audience* (January 12, 1966).

What was the key difference between Vatican II and all previous ecumenical councils?

The previous ecumenical councils formulated the doctrine of faith and morals in articles with the clearest possible assertions, and in concise canons with anathemas, to guarantee an unambiguous understanding of the true doctrine and protect the faithful from heretical influences within or outside the Church. Vatican II, however, chose not to do this.

What does anathema mean in Scripture?

In the Old Testament, it means "to cut off" or separate (*haram* in Hebrew), indicating a person or thing condemned to be exterminated or forbidden to make use of. In the New Testament, *anathema* (from Greek) entails the loss of goods or exclusion from the society of the faithful, e.g.: "If anyone preach to you a gospel besides that which you have received, let him be anathema" (Gal 1:9*).

What does anathema mean in the Church's dogmatic pronouncements?

Every ecumenical council from Nicea I to Vatican I worded its dogmatic canons: "If anyone says... let him be anathema," to clearly proscribe grave errors in faith.

Is the menace of the anathema an act of charity both toward the erring and the rest of the faithful?

Yes. "It is an act of the greatest charity toward all the faithful, comparable to preventing a dangerous disease from infecting innumerable people. By isolating the bearer of infection, we protect the bodily health of others; by the anathema, we protect their spiritual health.... And more: a rupture of communion with the heretic in no way implies that our obligation of charity toward him ceases. No, the Church prays also for heretics; the true Catholic who knows a heretic personally prays ardently for him and would never cease to impart all kinds of help to him."[93]

In our day, what is the most insidious enemy of the Church's constant Tradition?

It is *Modernism*, against which the Magisterium of the Church has warned: "The monstrous errors of 'Modernism'... Our Predecessor rightly declared to be 'the synthesis of all heresies,' and solemnly condemned.... As the plague is not yet entirely stamped out, but lurks here and there in hidden places, We exhort all to be carefully on their guard against any contagion of the evil.... Nor do We merely desire that Catholics should shrink from the errors of Modernism, but also from the tendencies or what is called the 'spirit' of Modernism. Those who are infected by that spirit develop a keen dislike for all that savors of antiquity and become eager searchers after novelties in everything: in the way in which they carry out religious functions, in the ruling of Catholic institutions, and even in private exercises of piety. Therefore, it is Our will that the law of our forefathers should still be held sacred: 'Let there be no innovation; keep to what has been handed down.'"[94]

---

[93] Dietrich von Hildebrand, *The Charitable Anathema* (Harrison: Roman Catholic Books, 1993), 1. In the traditional Holy Friday Liturgy the Church also prays explicitly for heretics; unfortunately, the new Pauline Missal omits this prayer.

[94] Pope Benedict XV, *Ad Beatissimi Apostolorum*, 25.

Can a layman's *sensus fidei* ("sense of the Faith") ever lead him to reject a teaching of the clergy?

Yes. Alerted by his *sensus fidei*, the lay faithful may deny assent even to the teachings of legitimate pastors when these appear evidently contrary to right faith or morals, or undermine their integrity. St. Paul warned even of bishops who would teach error as "ravening wolves" (Acts 20:29*), formulating this principle for both clergy and lay faithful: "Even if we or an angel from heaven should proclaim to you a gospel contrary to what we proclaimed to you, let that one be accursed! As we have said before, so now I repeat, if anyone proclaims to you a Gospel contrary to what you received, let that one be accursed [anathema sit]!" (Gal 1:8–9).

Isn't this sinful disobedience, dissent from the Magisterium, and a form of Protestantism?

No. Rather than treat oneself as the ultimate criterion of truth (which *is* a form of Protestantism), the faithful Catholic faced with a disturbing yet "authorized" teaching merely defers to the superior authority of the universal, perennial, traditional teachings of the Church, rejecting what departs from it.

When and how may clergy or laity legitimately resist or admonish their superiors—even a pope?

"Just as it is licit to resist the pontiff that aggresses the body, it is also licit to resist the one who aggresses souls or who disturbs civil order, or, above all, who attempts to destroy the Church. I say that it is licit to resist him by not doing what he orders and by preventing his will from being executed; it is not licit, however, to judge, punish, or depose him, since these acts are proper to a superior."[95]

---

[95] St. Robert Bellarmine, *De Romano Pontifice*, bk. 2, chap. 29.

Are there historical examples of such lawful resistance to ambiguous and erroneous teachings of the Church's legitimate pastors?

Yes. Providence has given a clear example in the Arian crisis of the fourth century, when heresy infected almost the entire episcopate and yet the lay people remained faithful to the traditional Catholic Faith. "In that time of immense confusion, the divine dogma of Our Lord's divinity was proclaimed, enforced, maintained, and (humanly speaking) preserved, far more by the *Ecclesia docta* [laity] than by the *Ecclesia docens* [hierarchy].... The body of the episcopate was unfaithful to its commission, while the body of the laity was faithful to its baptism.... At one time the pope, at other times the patriarchal, metropolitan, and other great sees, at other times general councils, said what they should not have said, or did what obscured and compromised revealed truth; while, on the other hand, it was the Christian people who, under providence, were the ecclesiastical strength of Athanasius, Hilary, Eusebius of Vercellae, and other great solitary confessors, who would have failed without them."[96]

May Catholics propose emendations or corrections of evidently ambiguous or erroneous statements or commands of a pope or ecumenical council?

Yes. The faithful "have the right, indeed at times the duty, in keeping with their knowledge, competence, and position, to manifest to the sacred pastors their views on matters which concern the good of the Church. They have the right also to make their views known to others of Christ's faithful, but in doing so they must always

---

[96] St. John Henry Cardinal Newman, *The Arians of the Fourth Century* (London: Longmans, Green, and Co., 1908), 465–466.

respect the integrity of faith and morals, show due reverence to the pastors, and take into account both the common good and the dignity of individuals."[97]

Why does the Roman Pontiff alone possess supreme authority in the Church?

Because, as Successor of St. Peter, he has the primacy which Our Lord conferred on Peter, the Prince of the Apostles (see Mt 16:17–19; Jn 21:15–17).

What is this primacy of the pope with regard to doctrine?

He is the principal teacher, guardian, and defender of the revealed truths. It belongs to him to: 1. Uphold what God has revealed to be believed, done, and avoided; 2. Condemn errors contrary to this divine revelation, contained in the apostolic doctrine he has received; 3. Be the visible sign and principle of the unity of faith and communion of the episcopate and the faithful.[98]

Is the pope infallible — that is, unable to teach error?

The pope is assisted by manifold graces for teaching the truth of Christ in his daily ministry, which is usually not infallible. When he teaches *ex cathedra* (from the Chair), he exercises the Church's charism of infallibility and is preserved free from error in that teaching.[99]

---

[97] *Code of Canon Law*, can. 212, §3.
[98] See Council of Vatican I, *Pastor Aeternus*, prooemium.
[99] See Council of Vatican I, *Dei Filius* and *Pastor Aeternus*.

How does infallibility differ from impeccability?

Infallibility is the impossibility of deceiving the Church by definitively binding it to a false doctrine, whereas *impeccability* is the impossibility of offending God and harming others by personal sin. The pope is infallible under limited conditions, but not impeccable.

Is papal infallibility a license to introduce new teachings?

No. The pope is bound scrupulously to obey the Catholic Faith transmitted to him by the perennial teaching of the Church, to keep this Faith intact, and to defend it. "The Holy Spirit was promised to the Successors of Peter not so that they might, by His revelation, make known some new doctrine, but that, by His assistance, they might religiously guard and faithfully expound the revelation or Deposit of Faith transmitted by the apostles."[100]

What makes a particular papal teaching *ex cathedra* and thus infallible?

The teaching must be: 1. Concerning a matter of faith or morals; 2. Addressed to the universal Church; 3. Proposed in virtue of the pope's supreme apostolic office; 4. Formulated as a final and binding definition.

What of those popes that have taught errors in the past?

No pope has ever taught—or could ever teach—an error by *ex cathedra* pronouncement. However, like any bishop, a pope may resist the grace of his office and possibly teach doctrinal errors in

---

[100] Council of Vatican I, *Pastor Aeternus*, chap. 4.

his daily, ordinary, and non-definitive assertions, i.e., outside of *ex cathedra* pronouncements.

Why has Christ made the pope infallible only in clearly determined circumstances, rather than continuously?

So that Christians would not divinize popes and give them the same credence and obedience that is owed only to the God-Man Jesus Christ, who is "head over all" (Eph 1:22*).

Do bishops have the power to teach and govern the faithful?

Yes. They are successors of the apostles by divine right, just as the pope is the Successor of St. Peter, chief of the apostles.

What powers do bishops have in their own dioceses?

They hold full legislative, administrative, and judiciary power; i.e., they have, within their respective dioceses, the same direct, complete, and personal power that the pope exercises over the whole Church, although they cannot eliminate, omit, or change what has been promulgated for the universal Church. "Bishops, as successors of the apostles, receive from the Lord, to whom was given all power in heaven and on earth, the mission to teach all nations and to preach the Gospel to every creature, so that all men may attain to salvation by faith, baptism, and the fulfillment of the commandments."[101]

---

[101] Council of Vatican II, *Lumen Gentium*, 24.

How do the bishops receive their canonical mission in the Church?

"By legitimate customs that have not been revoked by the supreme and universal authority of the Church, or by laws made or recognized by that authority, or directly through the Successor of Peter himself; and if the latter refuses or denies apostolic communion, such bishops cannot assume any office."[102]

Is the bishop a vicar of the pope, likened to a branch manager of a multinational corporation?

No. "The power of the Supreme Pontiff by no means detracts from that ordinary and immediate power of episcopal jurisdiction by which bishops, who have succeeded to the place of the apostles by appointment of the Holy Spirit, tend and govern individually the particular flocks which have been assigned to them."[103]

Then a bishop is not a mere representative of the pope?

No. "Although bishops do not receive plenary, universal, or supreme authority, they are not to be looked upon as mere representatives of the Roman Pontiffs. They exercise a power truly their own and are the ordinary pastors of the people whom they govern."[104]

Is it strictly necessary for bishops to gather and govern as collective bodies?

No. As true pastors, each bishop is charged by God to feed and govern the particular flock entrusted to him. Although collaboration among bishops is helpful at times, by divine law each bishop

---

[102] Council of Vatican II, *Lumen Gentium*, 24.
[103] Council of Vatican I, *Pastor Aeternus*, chap. 3.
[104] Pope Leo XIII, *Satis Cognitum*, 52.

is the shepherd in his own diocese; he is the teacher of the Faith and a loving father in Christ to his own people (see 1 Cor 4:15).

What is "collegiality"?
Collegiality is a general term for collaboration between bishops, especially when they are gathered in an ecumenical council or in other councils.

Does a false understanding of collegiality pose a danger for the Church?
Yes. It can lead to viewing Church governance as a democratic or egalitarian parliament, rather than the monarchical hierarchy established by Christ the King. It would diminish the supreme authority of the pope over the entire Church, and the local authority of each bishop in his own see.

How should collegiality be rightly exercised in the Church?
A moral collegiality of charity and mutual cooperation aids in the apostolic work of bishops, whereas a juridical or bureaucratic collegiality as found in today's Bishops' Conferences—one of endless meetings and collective policy-making—has already tended to diminish the bishop's sense of personal responsibility and ministry to his particular flock.

What is "synodality"?
Synodality is a novel pastoral model in which bishops are encouraged to gather regularly for dialogue with each other, their priests and faithful, and various interest groups from inside and outside the Church, about ecclesiastical or humanitarian matters.

Is synodality a positive development for the mission of the Church?

At present, it has borne no fruit in apostolic commitment of preaching the Catholic Faith to all nations or the conversion of non-Catholics, and has generally consumed significant time and resources that could be better spent for prayer and preaching, as St. Peter advised: "We will give ourselves continually to prayer, and to the ministry of the word" (Acts 6:4*). Such meetings also risk undermining the constitution of the Church, giving the false impression of the Church as a democratic institution, and needlessly exposing her ministers to secular pressure groups.

ERRORS ABOUT GRACE

Do rational creatures need a special divine grace called *lumen gloriae* to be elevated to the Beatific Vision?

Yes. The Church has solemnly condemned the error that "any intellectual nature in its own self is naturally blessed, and the soul does not need the *light of glory* raising it to see God and to enjoy Him beatifically."[105]

Does man have a right to the Beatific Vision in heaven?

No. The Beatific Vision is not due to man's nature as such, but remains a divine gift. Pope Pius V condemned the heresy of Michael Baius, that "the exaltation of human nature into the partnership of the divine nature was due to the integrity of the

---

[105] Council of Vienne, Session 3, *Errors of the Beghards and Beguines Concerning the State of Perfection* (May 6, 1312).

first condition, and hence it must be called nature, and not supernature."[106] Pope Pius XII likewise taught: "Others destroy the gratuity of the supernatural order, since God, they say, cannot create intellectual beings without ordering and calling them to the Beatific Vision."[107]

Is faith a necessary virtue for salvation?

Yes. "The one who does not believe will be condemned" (Mk 16:16). Faith is an absolutely necessary condition for the reception of sanctifying grace, without which no one can be saved.

Is habitual faith sufficient for salvation?

Habitual faith, an interior disposition communicated by baptism, is sufficient for those who do not have the use of reason; but those who have use of their reason must have *actual* faith to be saved, meaning that we must submit our intellect and will to God by our own personal choice.

To be saved, what truths must we believe with explicit faith?

We must at least believe and profess: 1. The existence of one God, who is a Rewarder of our works in eternity; 2. The mystery of the Blessed Trinity; 3. The Incarnation of the Son of God for our salvation.[108]

What are two general errors about divine grace?

1. So exalting the natural powers of man as to make divine grace unnecessary, as *Pelagianism* and *naturalism*; 2. So exalting divine

---

[106] Bull *Ex Omnibus Afflictionibus* (October 1, 1576).
[107] *Humani Generis*, 26.
[108] See ST II-II, q. 2, a. 8, c.

grace as to make man's free cooperation unnecessary or impossible, as *Lutheranism, Calvinism, Baianism,* and *Jansenism.*

What is naturalism?

An exclusion, and sometimes a negation, of the entire supernatural order. Naturalism ultimately leads to a complete Anti-Christianity, because it holds man and nature as self-sufficient.

How does the Magisterium of the Church describe naturalism?

"The fundamental doctrine of the naturalists, which they sufficiently make known by their very name, is that human nature and human reason ought in all things to be mistress and guide.... They deny that anything has been taught by God; they allow no dogma of religion or truth which cannot be understood by the human intelligence, nor any teacher who ought to be believed by reason of his authority."[109]

Conversely, what errors exalt divine grace to the detriment of our cooperation?

In addition to those of Luther and Calvin, the Church condemned the errors of Belgian theologian Michael Baius (+1589), Dutch bishop Cornelius Jansen (+1638), and French Jansenist theologian Paschal Quesnel (+1719), including the notions that "free will, without the help of God's grace, is valid only to sin,"[110] and that

---

[109] Pope Leo XIII, *Humanum Genus*, 12.
[110] Pope Pius V, *Ex Omnibus Afflictionibus.*

the fallen soul has "a general impotence for labor, for prayer, and for every good work."[111]

What is the most common error about divine grace today?

Neo-Pelagianism, the notion that men will be saved merely by their morally good deeds, apart from cooperation with divine grace and saving faith.

Does mere human existence enable man to reach perfection?

No. Man must become Christian, because he needs the help of God's grace for his: 1. Reason to understand the essential truths of faith without admixture of error; 2. Will to act rightly toward eternal life, his true perfection; 3. Passions to be well-ordered and in harmony with reason.

Are there erroneous forms of prayer that must be avoided?

Yes. Any path of prayer that seeks union with God apart from the sacred humanity of Jesus Christ, the Incarnate Word, is incomplete and deceptive: "No one comes to the Father, but by Me" (Jn 14:6).

May we practice "Christianized" forms of Yoga, Zen, or other pagan prayer forms?

No. Forms of prayer that are foreign to Christianity may not be safely practiced, as these are inherently linked to false worship and the deceptions of the devil. "What agreement hath the temple of God with idols?" (2 Cor 6:16*).

---

[111] Pope Clement XI, Dogmatic Constitution *Unigenitus* (September 8, 1713).

Errors about Religious Liberty

How must the Kingship of Christ be acknowledged?
Individually, by our choice to believe His doctrine and obey His commands; 2. *Collectively,* by families and nations living in accord with the same doctrine and moral precepts; 3. *Privately,* by progressing in the interior life of holiness; 4. *Publicly,* by imitating, obeying, and adoring our King in all external actions.

Are there disastrous consequences if Christ is excluded from political life?
Yes. "With God and Jesus Christ excluded from political life, with authority derived not from God but from man, the very basis of that authority has been taken away.... The result is that human society is tottering to its fall, because it no longer has a secure and solid foundation."[112]

What error affirms the radical principle of "separation of Church and State"?
It is generally called Liberalism. Because of its fundamental inability to recognize the true goal of human life in virtue and beatitude, Liberalism cannot build a society that serves this goal. Instead, it promotes individualism to the harm of the common good, foments unrestricted license in speech and press, and results in attacks on the one true religion.

---

[112] Pope Pius XI, *Quas Primas,* 18.

Isn't "religious liberty" a fundamental and inalienable human right?

No. Every *right,* or moral ability to do something according to law, is given to man only for true actions. But error and falsehood, especially in matters of religion, is evil in itself, and therefore does not establish the title of lawful right.[113] While everyone has the natural right to not be coerced to practice a religion, no man has the right—even a merely civil right—to offend God by choosing a moral evil, or by practicing or promoting religious error.[114] God has given all men the natural right to choose only the good and the true, which is the only proper use of their freedom.

Has the constant Magisterium of the Church maintained an inalienable and natural right in man to propagate a false religion?

No. Pope Leo XIII thus recapitulated the traditional doctrine of the Church: "Liberty is a power perfecting man, and hence should have truth and goodness for its object. But the character of goodness and truth cannot be changed at option. These remain ever one and the same, and are no less unchangeable than nature itself. If the mind assents to false opinions, and the will chooses and follows after what is wrong, neither can attain its native fullness, but both must fall from their native dignity into an abyss of corruption. Whatever, therefore, is opposed to virtue and truth may not rightly be brought temptingly before the eye of man, much less sanctioned by the favor and protection of the law."[115]

---

[113] See Bishop Javier Miguel Ariz Huarte, *Acta Synodalia Sacrosancti Concilii Oecumenici Vaticani Secundi*, vol. 3, per. 3, pt. 2, Congregationes Generales LXXXIII–LXXXIX, Città del Vaticano 1974, 627.

[114] See Pope Leo XIII, *Libertas Praestantissimum.*

[115] Encyclical *Immortale Dei*, 32.

Is there any legitimate civil right to immunity in exercising and spreading a false religion?

No. Although such affirmations have been made even by Church authorities in our time,[116] no one has a universal, positive, and natural right to practice whatever he perceives as "religion." Any civil rights to the same are likewise a grave error, as all ethically valid civil laws must be in harmony with the positive divine will, expressed in divine revelation and in the natural law. Civil laws promoting the liberty to offend God through the propagation of false religions cannot be a valid expression of or rooted in human nature.

What is the general modern error about conscience?

"When men advocate the rights of conscience, they in no sense mean the rights of the Creator, nor the duty to Him, in thought and deed, of the creature; but the right of thinking, speaking, writing, and acting, according to their judgment or their humor, without any thought of God at all.... Conscience is a stern monitor, but in this century it has been superseded by a counterfeit:... It is the right of self-will."[117]

---

[116] As, e.g., in the following affirmations of Vatican II: "This [religious] freedom means that... no one is to be forced to act in a manner contrary to his own beliefs, whether privately or publicly, whether alone or in association with others, within due limits.... The right to this immunity continues to exist even in those who do not live up to their obligation of seeking the truth and adhering to it and the exercise of this right is not to be impeded, provided that just public order be observed" (*Dignitatis Humanae* [December 7, 1965], 2).

[117] St. John Henry Cardinal Newman, "Letter to the Duke of Norfolk," in *Certain Difficulties Felt by Anglicans in Catholic Teaching* (London: Longmans, Green, and Co., 1900), 2:250.

Does an invincibly erroneous conscience in matters of religion establish a lawful right?

No. An invincibly erroneous conscience excuses from sin when one violates divine law as a result of such an error, but can never establish a right to such violations. Rights are established according to strictly objective criteria, not in the subjective order; therefore, he who, out of an erroneous conscience, acts contrary to the divine law and does not embrace the Catholic Faith, does not acquire the right to propagate doctrines contrary to revealed truth.[118]

Does a false notion of religious freedom easily make the individual conscience a source of rights and duties in religious matters?

Yes, as it subordinates the objective to the subjective order. In truth, the dictates of the subjective conscience must submit to the objective truths and morals established by God and sufficiently manifested to man either by nature or revelation.[119]

Has the Church condemned the theory of unlimited private choice in religion?

Yes. Pope Pius IX formally condemned the following opinions: "Every man is free to embrace and profess that religion which, guided by the light of reason, he shall consider true,"[120] and, "Men

---

[118] See Bishop Javier Miguel Ariz Huarte, *Acta Synodalia Sacrosancti Concilii Oecumenici Vaticani Secundi*, vol. 3, per. 3, pt. 2, Congregationes Generales LXXXIII–LXXXIX, Città del Vaticano 1974, 627.

[119] See Bishop Benigno Chiriboga, *Acta Synodalia Sacrosancti Concilii Oecumenici Vaticani Secundi*, vol. 3, per. 3, pt. 2, Congregationes Generales LXXXIII–LXXXIX, Città del Vaticano 1974, 647.

[120] *Syllabus Errorum*, proposition 15, repeating the condemnation made in the Apostolic Letter *Multiplices inter* (June 10, 1851) and in the Allocution *Maxima Quidem* (June 9, 1862).

may, in the observance of any religion whatever, find the way of eternal salvation, and arrive at eternal salvation."[121]

What has the Magisterium called this theory of absolute liberty of conscience and religion?

It has been called "liberty of perdition." Pope Pius IX condemned the opinion "that liberty of conscience and worship is each man's personal right, which ought to be legally proclaimed and asserted in every rightly constituted society; and that a right resides in the citizens to an absolute liberty, which should be restrained by no authority whether ecclesiastical or civil, whereby they may be able openly and publicly to manifest and declare any of their ideas whatever, either by word of mouth, by the press, or in any other way.... [This is] preaching 'liberty of perdition' (St. Augustine, *Ep. 105 ad Donatistas*)."[122]

ERRORS ABOUT THE SACRAMENTS

What heretics have especially attacked the sacraments?

Chiefly the Protestants of the sixteenth century, and Modernists of the twentieth and the twenty-first centuries.

---

[121] *Syllabus Errorum*, proposition 16, repeating the condemnation made in the Encyclical *Qui Pluribus* (November 9, 1846) and in the Encyclical *Singulari Quidem* (March 17, 1856).
[122] Encyclical *Quanta Cura* (December 8, 1864), quoting Pope Gregory XVI, Encyclical *Mirari Vos* (August 15, 1832).

What were some particular errors of the Protestants?

The notions that: 1. Sacraments do not produce grace, but are only signs which excite our faith; 2. The number of the sacraments should be diminished; 3. Any person can confer the sacraments; 4. No sacraments imprint a character; 5. The sacramental ceremonies of the Catholic Church are entirely man-made, ridiculous, and contemptible.

Has the Church clearly refuted and condemned these errors?

Yes. These and many other related errors were condemned at the Council of Trent.

What are some particular errors of the Modernists?

The notions that: 1. Sacraments do not confer grace, but only affirm or celebrate the grace people already possess; 2. Sacraments are not the ordinary means of grace and salvation, because God intends for all to be saved, even without them; 3. Any manner of celebrating the sacraments is pleasing to God, so long as it arises from the local community.

What heresies denied the necessity of baptism for infants?

The Pelagian heresy denied the existence of original sin, and therefore asserted that infants do not need baptism; similarly, the Anabaptist heresy forbade baptism of children, saying that it was not necessary for salvation. But from the earliest times, the Church has baptized infants in order to confer grace, remove the effects of original sin, and ensure their salvation. The Council of Florence declared: "With regard to children, since the danger of death is often present and the only remedy available to them is the sacrament of baptism by which they are snatched away from the dominion of the devil and adopted as children of God, she admonishes that sacred baptism is not to be deferred."[123]

What is Pentecostalism?

Present in the so-called "Charismatic Movement" or "Renewal in the Spirit," it is a new phenomenon — in a sense, even a new religion — resembling heresies like Montanism that emphasize charismatic, demonstrative, sentimental, and irrational religious experience. It has penetrated many Christian communities and even non-Christian religions, and presents a real spiritual danger in our time.

What are the dangers inherent to these movements?

They essentially equate religion with intuition, feeling, and irrational sentiment, ending in subjectivism and arbitrariness. Experience and emotion then become the measure of holiness and religious practice, also opening the door for demonic influence and deception. These movements often lack the reasonability and dignified disposition of awe that Catholics have always demonstrated before God's majesty.

May we seek Church renewal in a new, so-called "Pre-Constantinian" Catholicism?

No. Any authentic renewal must adhere faithfully to what Christ the Lord handed down to the apostles, and what has developed in the Church's constant teaching and prayer, without rupture, over two thousand years. It would be heretical to wish to erase the time from the Edict of Milan (313) to the beginning of Vatican II (1962),

---

[123] Bull of Union with the Copts *Cantate Domino*.

labeling the life of the Church during those seventeen centuries as "dark," "Constantinian," deprived of the guiding presence of the Holy Spirit.

What are the principal errors about the dogma of Christ's Real Presence in the Eucharist?

Those of: 1. *Berengarius* (+1088), who held that Christ is only figuratively present in the Eucharist; 2. Protestants like *Zwingli* (+1531) or *Calvin* (+1564), who denied the Real Presence entirely, while *Luther* (+1546) held it as only occurring during Holy Communion, and existing together with the substance of bread and wine (consubstantiation).

Is the dogmatic formula of transubstantiation still understandable and relevant?

Yes. The Tridentine formulation of this dogma is suitable for all men of all times, being a "perennially valid teaching of the Church"[124] and a divine truth that radically affects every aspect of life on earth: *Jesus Christ is truly with us.*

What are the major errors about the Sacrifice of the Mass?

Claims that it is: 1. Merely a spiritual offering of prayer and praise; 2. Merely a remembrance of Calvary; 3. A re-presentation of the Last Supper, not Christ's Passion; 4. A communal meal, not a true sacrifice; 5. Dependent for its validity or effectiveness on the participation of the congregation; 6. Not propitiatory for the living and the dead; 7. Able to be offered by someone other than an

---

[124] Pope John Paul II, Encyclical *Ecclesia de Eucharistia* (April 17, 2003), 15.

ordained priest; 8. Able to be offered with rubrics and ceremonies not determined by the universal Church.

Does the sacrificial action of the priest at Mass depend on the faith of the assembly?

No. It is achieved at the moment of the double consecration, "when Christ is made present upon the altar in the state of a victim, . . . performed by the priest and by him alone, as the representative of Christ and not as the representative of the faithful."[125]

Should the Eucharist itself be worshipped?

Yes. "If anyone saith, that, in the Holy Sacrament of the Eucharist, Christ, the only-begotten Son of God, is not to be adored with the worship, even external of *latria*; and is, consequently, neither to be venerated with a special festive solemnity, nor to be solemnly borne about in processions, according to the laudable and universal rite and custom of holy Church; or, is not to be proposed publicly to the people to be adored, and that the adorers thereof are idolators; let him be anathema."[126]

Does it respect the Church's tradition to receive Holy Communion in the hand?

No. The current practice of Communion in the hand is spiritually harmful and foreign to the Catholic liturgical patrimony, having been invented by Calvinists to signify their rejection of holy orders and transubstantiation.

---

[125] Pope Pius XII, Encyclical *Mediator Dei*, 92.
[126] Council of Trent, Session 13, *Decree on the Eucharist*, can. 6.

Why is Communion in the hand so spiritually harmful?

It violates: 1. The rights of Christ, failing in the proper reverence due to His Eucharistic fragments, sacred vessels, and ordained ministers; 2. Catholic faith and piety, weakening belief in and witness to the Incarnation and transubstantiation; 3. The necessary custody of consecrated hosts, which are increasingly stolen and abused.

Should the indult (special permission) for Communion in the hand be continued?

No. There is no supposed "pastoral need" or alleged "right of the faithful" that can justify danger to faith or sacrilege, when Our Eucharistic Lord has a right to the greatest possible reverence.

What ancient practice is sometimes invoked to defend Communion in the hand?

In some places during the first centuries, Holy Communion was placed on the palm of the right hand, sometimes covered with a *dominicale* (white cloth), after which the faithful bowed to take the host directly by mouth. The hand was washed before and after to purify it, so that no fragment would be lost. There is no evidence that this practice was ever universal in the Church.[127]

---

[127] St. Cyril of Jerusalem's observation (see *Cat. Myst.* 5, no. 21) that the faithful would touch the consecrated blood of Christ to their eyes was a bizarre instance, and not representative of the general Catholic practice. The views and practices of an individual Father of the Church are not infallible, and may diverge from the common tradition and practice of the universal Church.

Why did the Church eventually prohibit Communion in the hand?

An admirable consensus was already reached in East and West by the first millennium, when it was observed that conditions no longer existed to ensure the proper respect for the Eucharist, and the highest honors were increasingly and instinctively paid to this sacred mystery.

Does the Church deny Holy Communion to public sinners?

Yes. In her reverence for the Eucharist, care for the unity of her members, and concern for the sinner's salvation, the Church denies Communion to anyone in a public state of objectively grave sin; such as concubinage, adulterous cohabitation, public (especially political) support for abortion, same-sex civil unions, homosexual activity, etc.[128]

May a public sinner nonetheless present himself for Communion?

No. This is the damnable sin of unworthy Communion, "eating and drinking judgment" (cf. 1 Cor 11:29, 27). As St. John Chrysostom declared, "I too raise my voice, I beseech, beg, and implore that no one draw near to this sacred table with a sullied and corrupt conscience. Such an act, in fact, can never be called 'communion,' not even were we to touch the Lord's body a thousand times over, but 'condemnation,' 'torment,' and 'increase of punishment.'"[129]

---

[128] See *Code of Canon Law*, can. 915.
[129] *In Isaiam*, Hom. 6, no. 3, quoted in Pope John Paul II, *Ecclesia de Eucharistia*, 36.

May the Eucharist be administered to Protestants or the Orthodox?

No. As the sacrament of unity (see 1 Cor 10:17), the Eucharist "is properly the sacrament of those who are in full communion with the Church."[130] It may not be given to those who deny any truth of the Church's faith or her unity by formally adhering to any heretical or schismatic community. "It is the duty of all who heard Jesus Christ, if they wished for eternal salvation, not merely to accept His doctrine as a whole, but to assent with their entire mind to all and every point of it, since it is unlawful to withhold faith from God even in regard to one single point."[131]

Is it possible for women to receive holy orders?

No. By the will of God and the irreformable constitution of the Church, only baptized men are able to receive sacramental orders, as it configures them to the eternal priesthood of the God-Man, Jesus Christ, the Bridegroom of the Church His Bride, and enables them to represent Him sacramentally as a spiritual father.

What of those who clamor for the ordination of women as Catholic clergy?

They: 1. Oppose the divinely established order of the two sexes, each with its own specific mission; 2. Reject the hierarchical constitution of the Church; 3. Denigrate the unique dignity of Christian womanhood, consisting principally in motherhood, both physical and spiritual.

---

[130] *Catechism of the Catholic Church*, 1395.
[131] Pope Leo XIII, Encyclical *Satis Cognitum*, 8.

Why can't a woman be ordained a priest?

Because this would be: 1. Contrary to both Scripture and Tradition, as this was never done in the Old Law, nor in the New; 2. Inconsistent with the spousal meaning of priesthood, whereby a man represents and extends the presence of Christ the Bridegroom of the Church; 3. Opposed to the right ordering of the sexes, whereby "the head of every man is Christ, the head of a woman is her husband" (1 Cor 11:3), and no woman is "to teach or to have authority over men" (1 Tm 2:12); 4. Impossible, given the Church's infallible teaching that women cannot be ordained.

Has the Magisterium definitively rejected all possibility of women's ordination?

Yes. "In order that all doubt may be removed regarding a matter of great importance, a matter which pertains to the Church's divine constitution itself, in virtue of my ministry of confirming the brethren (cf. Lk 22:32*), I declare that the Church has no authority whatsoever to confer priestly ordination on women and that this judgment is to be definitively held by all the Church's faithful."[132]

May women nonetheless receive the order of deacon?

No. The sacrament of holy orders is one sacrament, conferred in three grades. The sacramental ordination of women as deacons would therefore contradict the whole Tradition of the universal Church, both Eastern and Western, and violate her God-given order, since the Council of Trent dogmatically defined: "The divinely

---

[132] Pope John Paul II, Apostolic Letter *Ordinatio Sacerdotalis* (May 22, 1994), 4.

established hierarchy is made up of bishops, priests, and ministers,"[133] i.e., at least also of deacons.

Does the Church have any power to ordain women to the sacramental diaconate?

No. The Church has no power to elevate or declare any non-sacramental ecclesiastical office (such as the historical "deaconess") to be part of the tripartite sacrament of holy orders.

Should women receive minor orders, or exercise the service of lector or acolyte?

No. The unbroken and universal practice of the Church prohibited women from the liturgical service of lector and acolyte, and canon law likewise prohibited women from receiving minor orders or the ministry of reader and acolyte, as these are rooted in the sacramental diaconate. In the absence of the minor orders, only male faithful fulfill the functions of lector ("reader") or acolyte ("altar server"), because the male sex is the last link joining the inferior liturgical or deputy ministers with the diaconate at the symbolic level: the male sex of inferior ministers reflects the Levitical or diaconal liturgical ministry, which in turn was strictly ordered and subordinated to the priesthood—reserved by God exclusively for men in the Old Covenant, and continuing in the New, as attested by the constant and universal canonical and liturgical Tradition of the entire Church.

---

[133] Session 23, *Doctrine on the Sacrament of Holy Orders*, can. 6.

Is parental approval required for a couple to contract a valid marriage?

No. However, it is most advisable to seek the counsel of loving parents and prudent friends when choosing a worthy spouse.

Can the Church ever permit spouses to live apart from one another?

Yes. For a just cause, a local ordinary can permit spousal separation for up to six months at a time.[134] For certain grave causes, spouses may also be permitted to suspend or cease conjugal relations (separation from "bed") and cohabitation (separation from "board"), although the bond of marriage still persists.

What reasons could justify such a separation from bed and board?

1. Mutual consent for a just cause, there being no further obligations to children (e.g., desire to enter religious life); 2. Grave danger to soul or body; 3. Certainty that one of the parties has committed adultery.

In such cases, may Christians also seek a divorce in civil law?

Yes, when this is the only means of adequate self-defense; e.g., maintaining legal protection and provision for the innocent spouse or children. However, such civil action has no effect on the marriage bond, which is beyond the power of the state to dissolve.

---

[134] See *Code of Canon Law*, cann. 1151–1155.

Can those who divorce and later "remarry" another in civil law grow in grace and charity?

No. One who knowingly chooses to live as though married to a civil partner while their true spouse is still alive is a public adulterer, living in the state of mortal sin. They can receive neither sanctifying grace nor salvation until they repent and are reconciled to God.

May spouses use contraception?

No. The conjugal act is ordered to procreation and expresses total and mutual self-giving, for which reason it is called the *marital act*. To intentionally render this act infertile—whether by interruption, barrier, surgery, chemicals, or otherwise—corrupts its very nature, and changes it into an act against the order established by God the Creator.

May spouses contracept in order to practice responsible parenthood?

No. "Any action which either before, at the moment of, or after sexual intercourse is specifically intended to prevent procreation—whether as an end or as a means,"[135] is in itself "an offense against the law of God and of nature, and those who indulge in such are branded with the guilt of a grave sin."[136]

---

[135] Pope Paul VI, *Humanae Vitae*, 14.
[136] Pope Pius XI, *Casti Connubii*, 56.

May spouses agree to abstain from conjugal relations within marriage?

Yes. Abstaining from the marital act by mutual consent—whether permanently or for a time—has been practiced since apostolic times (see 1 Cor 7:5).

How is such periodic abstinence different from contraception?

Unlike contraceptive intercourse, conjugal relations during the periods of female infertility are not contrary to nature, and it is morally licit to confine oneself to these periods when there are serious reasons.

Is it possible to abuse this morally licit method of periodic abstinence?

Yes. Anything that admits of a legitimate use can also be abused, and periodic abstinence may be turned into a cloak for selfishness. "If the sincere intention of letting the Creator do His work freely is lacking, human selfishness will always be able to find new sophisms and expedients to silence consciences, if possible, and perpetuate the abuses... [that oppose] readiness to accept with joy and gratitude the priceless gifts of God, which are children, and in the number that pleases Him."[137]

Then the method of periodic abstinence can even become sinful?

Yes, when used with a *contraceptive mentality*, i.e., for selfish motives directed against the procreative end of marriage. "Taking advantage

---

[137] Pope Pius XII, *Address to the Directors of the Associations for Large Families of Rome and Italy* (January 20, 1958).

of the 'infertile periods' in conjugal coexistence can become a source of abuse.... By separating the natural method from the ethical dimension, one ceases to perceive the difference between it and the other 'methods' (artificial means)... as if it were only a question of a different form of contraception."[138]

Is it advisable to use the expression "Natural Family Planning"?

No. This sounds overly technical and bureaucratic, like an economic plan for grain production or cattle breeding. It is unworthy to apply the word *planning* to human persons, potential children of God and new citizens of heaven.

May spouses use artificial insemination, in vitro fertilization, or surrogate motherhood?

No. It is never permitted to separate human procreation from the conjugal union, and any action that divides the unitive and procreative end of the marital act is against the natural order established by God, and therefore, gravely sinful.

If one spouse dies, may the survivor marry again?

Yes. The marriage bond is dissolved by death: "A wife is bound to her husband as long as he lives. If the husband dies, she is free to be married to whom she wishes, only in the Lord" (1 Cor 7:39).

---

[138] Pope John Paul II, General Audience (September 5, 1984), 3–4.

Does the civil power have authority to redefine marriage in civil law?

No. Changing the nature of marriage is beyond the scope of any human power, and its redefinition in law is one of the greatest social evils of our time. Such initiatives must be strongly opposed by clergy and faithful of every rank.

Why is the redefinition of marriage in civil law such a great evil?

Governments that enact such measures — particularly those granting legal recognition to same-sex unions — are complicit in sins crying to heaven for vengeance, and place their nation on the path of moral and physical destruction.

May a so-called "same-sex marriage" in civil law ever be blessed by the Church?

No. Any unions that have the name of marriage without the reality of it are not capable of receiving the blessing of the Church, as these are contrary to natural and divine law.

May the Church nonetheless support so-called "civil unions" between persons of the same sex?

No. Even if such arrangements do not receive the name of "marriage" in law, they plainly imitate it — thus encouraging grave sin and causing serious scandal, which the Church can never approve or appear to condone.

Should persons in state-recognized same-sex unions be eligible to adopt children?

No. Their public rejection of natural and divine law renders them habitually unholy, unstable, and unfit to care for children, and organizations permitting such adoptions are complicit in grave sin, enacting a real moral violence against children.

May we ever attend the celebration of such unions?

No. To do so would be a failure in charity and justice, and cause serious scandal. "Woe to those that call evil good" (Is 5:20*), for, "if you do not warn him... the wicked man will die in his iniquity, and I will hold you responsible for his blood" (Ez 3:18*).

Errors about Morality

Is everyone able to fulfill the commandments of God?

Yes. God's grace is available to all, and with the assistance of divine grace, "I can do all things through Him who strengthens me" (Phil 4:13). The Church teaches infallibly: "If anyone says that the commandments of God are, even for one that is justified and constituted in grace, impossible to observe, let him be anathema."[139]

---

[139] Council of Trent, Session 6, *Decree on Justification*, can. 18.

Are some actions also objectively evil, i.e., always and absolutely evil?

Yes. Also called *intrinsically* evil, such acts "are not capable of being ordered to God and to the good of the person."[140] Examples include all direct violations of divine worship (e.g., idolatry, blasphemy), truth (e.g., lying, perjury), innocent human life (e.g., murder, abortion, euthanasia), and marriage (e.g., fornication, contraception).

In order to be good, do our acts need to be performed in the state of grace?

No. Even the wicked "know how to give good gifts" (Mt 7:11). However, we must be in the state of grace to perform supernaturally good acts, which alone merit the reward of grace.

What false moral systems are most common today?

1. *Determinism*, which denies the fact that man has free will, and so dissolves all moral responsibility; 2. *Consequentialism*, which declares all actions to be good if their intention is good or outcome desirable; 3. *Relativism*, which rejects all moral absolutes.

What new errors about morality are beginning to emerge?

The related notions that: 1. Man can never have sufficient knowledge to commit sin, or at least any grave sin; 2. A person who performs grave evils can still have a good "character" and even enter heaven, so long as his overall intention in life is good;[141] 3. God

---

[140] Pope John Paul II, Encyclical *Veritatis Splendor* (August 6, 1993), 80.

[141] Pope John Paul II condemned such *teleological* and *proportionalist* theories, which hold that it is impossible to qualify the deliberate choice of certain kinds of behavior or acts as "objectively evil," apart

does not offer sufficient grace for a person to perform a good act or avoid moral evil; 4. God may command evils in some situations, in view of some social or familial good.[142]

What are the chief errors with regard to the divine law today?

1. *Rabbinic Judaism*, which holds fidelity to the Mosaic Law as sufficient for salvation; 2. *Judaizing*, whereby Christians adopt Jewish ceremonies that have already been fulfilled and superseded by the coming of Christ, e.g., "seder meals" and ritual circumcision; 3. *Antinomianism*, which maintains that Christians are exempt from some or all obligations of the moral law; 4. *Moral liberalism*, which asserts that divine law in its immutable aspect of the Ten Commandments is an abstract ideal, impossible or harmful to observe in some concrete circumstances; 5. *Gradualism*, which asserts that people can be in right relationship with God and the state of grace by gradually becoming more "ethical," even while knowingly continuing in mortal sin.

Must human laws—whether in the family, nation, or Catholic Church—always be followed?

Yes, unless they are unjust. A law is unjust if it exceeds the jurisdiction of the legislator, gravely threatens the common good, or contradicts natural law or divine law; in such cases, it is an act of

---

from a consideration of the intention for which the choice is made or the totality of the foreseeable consequences of that act (see *Veritatis Splendor*, 79).

[142] These latter two errors have insinuated themselves even into recent papal documents regarding the case of couples living in adulterous unions; see Pope Francis, Apostolic Exhortation *Amoris Laetitia* (March 19, 2016), 295, 298, 301, and footnote 329.

violence rather than a true law. It is null and void, and need not be followed.[143]

What should we do when an ecclesiastical law is manifestly harmful?

Any law or command of an ecclesiastical superior—even the pope—that undermines or evidently harms the clarity or integrity of the Church's constant law of faith (lex credendi), morals (lex vivendi), or liturgy (lex orandi) must not be obeyed.

Aren't Catholics bound to obey the pope and other ecclesiastical superiors in all things?

No. Although the pope has universal and immediate jurisdiction over every Catholic, no one must obey him in all things without qualification: "Man is subject to God simply as regards all things, both internal and external, wherefore he is bound to obey Him in all things. On the other hand, inferiors are not subject to their superiors in all things, but only in certain things and in a particular way, in respect of which the superior stands between God and his subjects, whereas in respect of other matters the subject is immediately under God, by whom he is taught either by the natural or by the written law."[144]

What is the chief reason for such disobedience to ecclesiastical laws or commands?

"If the Faith were endangered, a subject ought to rebuke his prelate even publicly. Hence Paul, who was Peter's subject, rebuked him in public, on account of the imminent danger of scandal

---

[143] See ST I-II, q. 93, a. 3, rep. 2; q. 96, a. 4, rep. 2 and 3.
[144] ST II-II, q. 104, a. 5, rep. 2.

concerning faith."[145] St. Paul relates in Galatians 2:11: "When Cephas [Peter] came to Antioch I opposed him to his face, because he was to be blamed."

Is it necessary to keep all the commandments of God?

Yes. To willfully break any one of them in a grave matter is to commit a mortal sin.

Is a mere confidence in the mercy of God sufficient to remit sin?

No. The sinner must also have the dispositions expected of him by God.

Is cooperation with God's grace necessary for the forgiveness of sins?

Yes. Without the grace of God, the sinner is unable to move himself to repentance and faith by his own free will. Rather, he must freely assent to and cooperate with God's helping grace, which calls him to conversion. Hence, "Turn ye to Me,... and I will turn to you" (Zac 1:3*) reminds us of our liberty; and when we reply, "Convert us, O Lord, to Thee, and we shall be converted" (Lam 5:21*), we confess that we need the grace of God.[146]

What are the chief errors about the forgiveness of sins?

1. The despairing notion that some sins are too great to be forgiven by a loving God; 2. Denial of the Church's power to forgive sins; 3. Belief that man is incapable of truly committing sin; 4. Denial

---

[145] ST II-II, q. 33, a. 4, rep. 2.
[146] See Council of Trent, Session 6, *Decree on Justification*, chap. 5.

of all sin; 5. The heresy that claims forgiveness of sins is given by the sole imputation of Christ's justice, or that sins are merely covered up; 6. The heresy that in order to obtain forgiveness of sins, man must necessarily believe with certainty that his sins are forgiven; 7. The heresy that man, once forgiven, can sin no more, nor lose grace.[147]

Who is guilty of the sin of heresy?

Those who obstinately deny or willfully doubt a revealed truth. One who errs in good faith and is ready to submit to Church teaching as soon as he recognizes the truth (a merely "material" heretic) is not guilty of the sin of heresy.

What form of false worship has been repeatedly condemned by the Church?

Freemasonry. First explicitly condemned by Pope Clement XII in 1738, this pernicious error remains under the strongest censure.

What are the most recent judgments of the Church on Freemasonry?

The *Declaration on Masonic Associations* of the Congregation of the Doctrine of Faith (November 27, 1983) approved by Pope John Paul II, and the Document of the Dicastery for the Doctrine of the Faith *Ex Audientia Sanctissimi* (November 13, 2023) approved by Pope Francis. These maintain the Church's condemnation of Masonic associations, despite the fact that the new Code of Canon

---

[147] For these and other errors regarding the forgiveness of sins, see Council of Trent, Session 6, *Decree on Justification*.

Law does not mention them expressly, unlike the previous Code of 1917.[148]

Are Catholics ever permitted to be members of Masonic associations?

No. "The faithful who enroll in Masonic associations are in a state of grave sin and may not receive Holy Communion."[149]

Can individual cardinals or bishops approve of Freemasonry?

No. "It is not within the competence of local ecclesiastical authorities to give a judgment on the nature of Masonic associations which would imply a derogation from what has been decided [in the 1983 Declaration]."[150]

Who is guilty of the sin of false or idolatrous worship?

Those who actively participate in non-Catholic religious services, which worship God not as He desires; those who actively participate in syncretistic worship honoring pagan deities; those who worship inanimate objects or tokens of pagan mythology (e.g., symbols of the pagan Incan earth goddess Pachamama); Yoga and Reiki practitioners; those who worship nature itself, e.g., in the New Age movement or Gaianism (from the pagan Greek earth goddess Gaia), with terms like *Mother Nature* and *Mother Earth*.

---

[148] "Those who join a Masonic sect or other societies of the same sort, which plot against the Church or against legitimate civil authority, incur ipso facto an excommunication simply reserved to the Holy See" (can. 2335).

[149] Congregation for the Doctrine of the Faith, *Declaration on Masonic Associations* (November 27, 1983).

[150] Congregation for the Doctrine of the Faith, *Declaration on Masonic Associations*.

Has the Church warned against Gaianism and "Mother Earth" worship?

Yes. The Holy See identified their basic ideological principles as "the generalization of ecology as a fascination with nature and re-sacralization of the earth, Mother Earth or Gaia, with the missionary zeal characteristic of Green politics. The Earth's executive agent is the human race as a whole, and the harmony and understanding required for responsible governance is increasingly understood to be a global government, with a global ethical framework. The warmth of Mother Earth, whose divinity pervades the whole of creation, is held to bridge the gap between creation and the transcendent Father-God of Judaism and Christianity, and removes the prospect of being judged by such a Being."[151]

Why must Catholics be warned against Yoga and similar practices?

Yoga and similar practices (e.g., Zen meditation) are body and mind training derived from Hindu and/or Buddhist religions. "In their own context, the postures and exercises are determined by their specific religious purpose: they are, in themselves, steps that guide the practitioner toward an impersonal absolute. Even when they are carried out in a Christian environment, the intrinsic meaning of the gestures remains intact. Non-Christian forms of meditation are actually practices of deep concentration and not prayer. Through the relaxation exercises and the repetition of a *mantra* (sacred word)

---

[151] Pontifical Council for Culture, Pontifical Council for Interreligious Dialogue, *Jesus Christ the Bearer of the Water of Life: A Christian Reflection on the "New Age"* (2003), 2.3.1.

it is about plunging into the depth of one's own self in search of the anonymous absolute."[152]

Has the Church also warned against Reiki practices?

Yes. As a Japanese form of a so-called "energy healing," Reiki practitioners claim to transfer a "universal energy" through their palms to the patient, in order to encourage emotional or physical healing. "Without justification either from Christian faith or natural science, however, a Catholic who puts his or her trust in Reiki would be operating in the realm of superstition, the no-man's-land that is neither faith nor science. Superstition corrupts one's worship of God by turning one's religious feeling and practice in a false direction."[153] Some forms of Reiki also appeal for the assistance of angelic beings or "spirit guides," introducing further danger of exposure to the demonic.

Is the New Age movement merely a novel form of Gnosticism?

Yes. "We cannot delude ourselves that [New Age practice] will lead toward a renewal of religion. It is only a new way of practicing Gnosticism — that attitude of the spirit that, in the name of a profound knowledge of God, results in distorting His Word and replacing it with purely human words. Gnosticism never completely abandoned the realm of Christianity. Instead, it has always existed

---

[152] Norberto Rivera Carrera, Arzobispo Primado de México, *Instrucción pastoral sobre el New Age* (January 6, 1996), 33. See also Congregation for the Doctrine of the Faith, *Letter to the Bishops of the Catholic Church on Some Aspects of Christian Meditation* (October 15, 1989).

[153] Committee on Doctrine of the United States Conference of Catholic Bishops, *Guidelines for Evaluating Reiki as an Alternative Therapy* (March 25, 2009), 11.

side by side with Christianity, sometimes taking the shape of a philosophical movement, but more often assuming the characteristics of a religion or a para-religion in distinct, if not declared, conflict with all that is essentially Christian."[154]

Why are all neo-pagan globalist movements mortal enemies of the Catholic Church?

Because they maintain that "the New Age which is dawning will be peopled by perfect, androgynous beings who are totally in command of the cosmic laws of nature. In this scenario, Christianity has to be eliminated and give way to a global religion and a new world order."[155]

What are common sins that come about through the error of presumption?

If we: 1. Expect to be saved by our own efforts without the help of God's grace, as the heresy of *Pelagianism*; 2. Expect to be saved by faith alone and without works of penance or charity, as the heresy of *Martin Luther*; 3. Remain in sin and delay our conversion, trusting the divine mercy to be always available at our pleasure; 4. Willfully expose ourselves to near occasions of sin, confident in our strength to resist temptation.

Is scandal truly a grave sin in itself?

Yes. As it is a serious violation of charity to lead another to sin, *scandal*—i.e., any word, act, or omission (evil in itself or only in

---

[154] Pope John Paul II, *Crossing the Threshold of Hope* (New York: Random House, 1994), 90.
[155] Pontifical Council for Culture, Pontifical Council for Interreligious Dialogue, *Jesus Christ the Bearer of the Water of Life*, 3.5.

appearance) that leads another to sin—only becomes a venial sin when the matter is trifling.

What are the worst scandals?

1. Blasphemy or sacrilege; 2. False and heretical teachings; 3. Creation or distribution of media that oppose religion or morality; 4. Public exposition of obscenity and perversion in art; 5. Gossip, which often breeds hatred, desire for revenge, and lasting enmities; 6. Lustful and immodest speech, attire, or behavior.

What of Catholics in public office who act contrary to Church teaching?

This is at least a sin of negligence and scandal, for which they should be corrected by their pastors with a view to repentance and redressing the scandal caused. If they continue such acts, they must be publicly admonished for the sake of the salvation of their souls, and if still unrepentant and obstinate, be excluded from the reception of the sacraments.[156] The words of St. Ambrose apply to Catholics in any rank of public office: "The emperor is within the Church, not over the Church; a good emperor seeks the aid of the Church, he does not reject it."[157]

---

[156] "Those upon whom the penalty of excommunication or interdict has been imposed or declared, and others who obstinately persist in manifest grave sin, are not to be admitted to Holy Communion" (*Code of Canon Law*, can. 915).

[157] *Contra Auxentium*, no. 36.

What are the general errors about original sin?

Two extremes: 1. Those who deny original sin, as the Pelagians; 2. Those who overstate the condition or effects of original sin, as Luther, Calvin, Baius, and the Jansenists.

Did the sin of Adam injure him alone?

No. It affected all his descendants (excepting the Blessed Virgin Mary and Our Lord Jesus Christ). The Church condemned the errors of the Pelagians: "If anyone asserts that Adam's transgression injured him alone and not his descendants, or declares that certainly death of the body only, which is the punishment of sin, but not sin also, which is the death of the soul, passed through one man into the whole human race, he will do an injustice to God, contradicting the Apostle who says: 'Through one man sin entered in the world, and through sin death, and thus death passed into all men, in whom all have sinned' (Rom 5:12*)."[158]

What was the main error of Martin Luther regarding original sin?

Luther asserted the following heresy: "The nature of man is corrupted through and through by original sin and is damned within and without, in body and soul, and flees from God.... Spiritual powers are not only corrupted, but even totally destroyed in both men and devils, and nothing remains but a corrupted intellect and a will which is hostile and opposed to God at every point, which thinks and desires nothing but that alone which is contrary and opposed to God."[159]

---

[158] Council of Orange II (July 3, 529), can. 2.
[159] *De servo arbitrio* (*The Bondage of the Will*).

What are the Lutheran and Jansenist errors about the effects of original sin?

That sanctifying grace being an essential part of human nature, original sin must have the following consequences: 1. Man's absolute powerlessness in doing any good; 2. The necessity for him always to do evil, unless God intervenes to help. Man thus becomes no more than a lifeless object, devoid of natural goodness, that God moves at His will.

In the Lutheran and Jansenist theories, how can the "totally corrupted" nevertheless do good works?

They erroneously affirm that God's grace frees man from his powerlessness to do good by imposing itself on him, so that man can do a good work. The Church condemned this error: "If anyone saith, that man's free will moved and excited by God, by assenting to God exciting and calling, nowise cooperates toward disposing and preparing itself for obtaining the grace of justification; that it cannot refuse its consent, if it would, but that, as something inanimate, it does nothing whatever and is merely passive; let him be anathema."[160]

Why is lust said to be a disordered love of sexual pleasure?

Because sexual pleasure is not evil in itself; it becomes disordered only when sought outside of a valid marriage, or, within marriage, in the deliberate exclusion of its unitive or procreative dimensions.

---

[160] Council of Trent, Session 6, *Decree on Justification*, can. 4.

What vices can result from lust?

Lust leads to: 1. Blindness of mind, dulling and clouding our reason; 2. Inconstancy, especially in our good resolutions; 3. Self-love, unto the hatred of God; 4. Attachment to the things of this world; 5. Irreligion and atheism, as justifications for immoral behavior; 6. Despair.

Is the public normalization of sexual sin a clear mark of a decaying civilization?

Yes. As demonstrated many times throughout history, the society that normalizes any sexual sin—especially sodomy—is on the way to collective destruction.

What of those who habitually experience same-sex attractions?

One must distinguish between same-sex attraction, and homosexual behavior or acts. Involuntary sexual feelings, even if they are against nature, are not sinful unless one consents to them. Those who merely experience such attractions are to be treated with compassion, and are called to chastity and personal holiness no less than others.

Are sins of lust between persons of the same sex very grave?

Yes. Two persons of the same sex sin gravely when they seek venereal pleasure from each other, because homosexual acts are contrary to nature, reason, and divine law (see Lv 18:22; 20:13; Rom 1:24–28; 1 Cor 6:9–10; 1 Tm 1:10; and Jude 7).

May debilitating drugs or substances ever be used licitly?

Yes. When used for a recognized medical purpose, such as the alleviation of extreme physical pain, or as preparation for surgery, etc., in professionally recommended doses.

Is the recreational use of marijuana a sin of intoxication?

Yes. Due to its swift and immediate effect of impairing the intellect, marijuana may only be licitly used for genuine medicinal reasons under the supervision of a healthcare professional.

What kinds of superstition involve the worship of a false god?

Chiefly *idolatry*, which gives divine honor to any real or imagined creature, as in various forms of nature worship, e.g., the so-called "Pachamama" or "Mother Earth" ceremonies; all *divination*, *magic*, and *sorcery*, which seek the aid of demons or occult powers to learn what is hidden or exercise control, as in various forms of witchcraft, Wicca, and New Age practice.

Is the worship of false gods increasingly prevalent today?

Yes. As men abandon the only true worship of God in Christ, they increasingly revert to the errors of ancient paganism, or worship bodily health, power, nature, the Earth, and pleasure as their gods.

What kinds of superstition involve undue worship of the true God?

False worship, which contains something contrary to natural truth or divine revelation, as when false revelations are maintained;

impious worship, as when a man-centered worship is established in violation of the Church's constant liturgical tradition.

Is it sinful for Catholics to actively participate in the worship services of heretical sects or other false religions?

Yes. Any non-Catholic prayer service, whose content contradicts the Catholic Faith, constitutes *false worship*. By actively participating in such worship, we: 1. Refuse to worship God in the manner He desires; 2. Assent to the errors proclaimed there; 3. Fail in charity toward the erring; 4. Scandalize the faithful; 5. Endanger our own faith.

May we attend a non-Catholic religious service for reasons other than joining their prayer?

Even passive attendance at such services (e.g., weddings, funerals) is generally discouraged, but may be permitted if: 1. There is a very serious reason to attend; 2. We do not engage in the prayer or rite itself; 3. Any potential scandal is mitigated; 4. All danger to our faith is precluded.

Why do man-centered forms of worship violate the Church's constant liturgical tradition?

Because only "the received and approved rites of the Church"[161] offer to God the worship that He has prescribed, and only her constant liturgical custom best safeguards the truly God-centered form of worship.

---

[161] Pope Pius IV, Bull *Iniunctum Nobis* (November 13, 1565); see also the Council of Trent, Session 7.

Should we avoid a Mass in which liturgical abuses will foreseeably occur?

Yes. The presence of a valid Eucharist notwithstanding, ceremonies with liturgical abuses are objectively contrary to the divine and apostolic tradition, displeasing to God, scandalous, and often dangerous to faith.

Should we attend a Mass with liturgical abuses to fulfill our Sunday obligation?

This depends on the gravity of such abuses in each place. If a Sunday Mass would include practices like dances, heresies in preaching, or other serious liturgical abuses, we may not be obliged to attend such a Mass, even if it were the only one available in our vicinity, because we cannot be obliged to place ourselves or our families in a near occasion of danger to faith.

In this specific case, would we violate the third commandment?

No. The obligation to attend Sunday Mass is an ecclesiastical and not a divine law, and therefore subject to exemption and dispensation. If a Sunday Mass with liturgical abuses were the only available option, we should sanctify the Sunday in some other way; and in this way we are keeping the third commandment.

May a bishop ever suspend the obligation to attend Sunday Mass in his diocese?

No. He may remind the faithful of those circumstances in which the obligation ceases to bind, but because this is a universal law for Catholics based on divine law, it is beyond his authority (and spiritually and pastorally detrimental for his flock) to suspend the obligation itself.

May a pope or bishop prohibit the public offering of Mass for any cause?

No. As a divine institution and the common good of the entire Church, Holy Mass may only be prohibited in a particular place and time as an extreme measure of canonical punishment through interdict, and only for the most serious ecclesiastical crimes.

May the clergy ever prohibit rites of public worship due to concerns about public health?

No. The prohibition of divine worship or the sacraments in the name of public health is a violation of the rights of God and the faithful, as well as a subordination of the Church's supreme law — the salvation of souls[162] — to the care of bodies.

Must we comply with the prohibition of traditional Catholic liturgical rites?

No. "What earlier generations held as sacred, remains sacred and great for us too, and it cannot be all of a sudden entirely forbidden or even considered harmful. It behooves all of us to preserve the riches which have developed in the Church's faith and prayer, and to give them their proper place."[163] The rites of venerable antiquity form a sacred and constitutive part of the common patrimony of the Church, and not even the highest ecclesiastical authority has power to proscribe them.[164]

---

[162] *Salus animarum suprema lex*, "the salvation of souls is the supreme law" (*Code of Canon Law*, can. 1752).
[163] Pope Benedict XVI, Letter to the Bishops Accompanying the Apostolic Letter, "Summorum Pontificum" (July 7, 2007).
[164] As the medieval Papal Oath declared: "I shall keep inviolate the discipline and ritual of the Church, just as I found and received it handed down by my Predecessors."

May the civil power prohibit Catholic worship in the interest of public health?

No. States have power to issue general sanitary measures, which should be observed unless unreasonable. However, a general prohibition of Catholic worship would exceed the bounds of the civil power, and violate the divine rights of God and His Church.

Must we comply with civil mandates to undergo objectionable medical procedures?

No. "Public magistrates have no direct power over the bodies of their subjects," and because the state exists for the welfare of citizens, "where no crime has taken place,... [it] can never directly harm or tamper with the integrity of the body."[165]

What if such procedures are intended to protect the health of the general population?

Praiseworthy intentions notwithstanding, such initiatives are a form of medical violence and thus of tyranny. They may be justly opposed by citizens as such.

May we knowingly use medical products derived from fetal stem cells?

No. The development of such products cooperates in the abominable crimes of child-murder and organ theft, which currently drive the abortion and fetal industries. The knowing use of such products — e.g., abortion-tainted vaccines — involves the grave omission of a firm and public protest against such evils, and conscious consumption of the products of these inhuman

---

[165] Pope Pius XI, Encyclical *Casti Connubii* (December 31, 1930).

"industries" cooperates in the instrumentalization of the bodies of murdered children.

Does the principle of "double effect" justify the use of such products?

No. The principle of *double effect*—foreseeing two simultaneous effects from the same act: one undesired evil and one intended good—requires that our action itself be good, or at least morally neutral. While medicating to protect one's health is a moral good in the abstract, using an *abortion-tainted product* to do so is wrong in itself, vitiated by the circumstance of its creation: it came directly from the abuse and murder of children, and may even contain remnants of their tiny bodies. Therefore, the principle does not apply.

Has the Magisterium categorically and uncompromisingly condemned any use of fetal tissues of murdered unborn children?

Yes. "The use of human embryos or fetuses as an object of experimentation constitutes a crime against their dignity as human beings who have a right to the same respect owed to a child once born, just as to every person. This moral condemnation also regards procedures that exploit living human embryos and fetuses—sometimes specifically 'produced' for this purpose by in vitro fertilization—either to be used as 'biological material' or as providers of organs or tissue for transplants in the treatment of certain diseases. The killing of innocent human creatures, even if carried out to help others, constitutes an absolutely unacceptable act."[166]

---

[166] Pope John Paul II, *Evangelium Vitae*, 63.

What forms of legalized murder have become all too common in many societies?

1. *Abortion*, which intentionally destroys a child in the womb by chemical, surgical, or other means; 2. *Contraception*, which poses some temporary or permanent sterilizing obstacle to the conception of new life, and often causes abortion as well; 3. *Euthanasia*, which ends the life of the sick, handicapped, or elderly; 4. *In vitro fertilization* (IVF) methods, which inevitably lead to the destruction of cryopreserved (frozen) embryos; 5. *Political vengeance*, in which political prisoners and so-called "enemies of the state" are put in camps and even executed without due process of just laws.

What of politicians who advocate for any form of legalized murder?

They are complicit in grave sin, and may be publicly opposed. If they profess to be Catholic, they should be admonished by the Church's pastors, suitably punished in canon law if obstinate and unrepentant, and not admitted to Holy Communion until they have repented and repaired the scandal.[167]

What of those who commit sins of murder while claiming good intentions?

The desire to limit suffering and remove inconvenience is increasingly common in materialistic societies, which have lost sight of the redemptive value of suffering. Even so, no claim of good intentions can ever justify murder, and those who commit it — whether

---

[167] See *Code of Canon Law*, can. 915.

by direct action or omission—are guilty of grave sin. The end does not justify the means (see Rom 3:8).

May ordinary care of the sick ever be legitimately discontinued?

No. Even if death appears imminent, ordinary means of care should always be given to the suffering in our midst. In principle, this includes the obligation to provide medically assisted nutrition and hydration for those who cannot eat or drink by themselves.

Are the medical criteria for "brain death" sufficient to determine if someone is truly dead?

No. The body-soul union of the human person is not reducible to the level of brain function or cerebral cortex activity; if it were, the unborn or severely disabled could not be considered living human persons, contrary to what God has clearly affirmed (see Ps 139:15–16; Jer 1:5; Is 49:1; and Gal 1:15). As long as any vital functions continue, the rational soul is present,[168] and therefore a person is present, with all his personal rights.

---

[168] "The opinion which posits only one principle of life in man, that is, the rational soul, from which the body also receives all movement and life and sense, is the most common in the Church of God, and according to the most approved theologians it seems to be connected in such a way with the dogma of the Church, that it is the legitimate and only true interpretation, and therefore cannot be denied without error in faith" (Pope Pius IX, Apostolic Letter *Dolore Haud Mediocri* [April 30, 1860]).

Is it permissible to undergo medical treatments designed to contradict our biological sex?

No. Being contrary to natural and divine law, it is gravely sinful to alter one's body with chemicals or mutilation to express a different bodily sex than that which has been given by God.

What of the felt need to "self-identify" as a different sex than that given by God?

The causes of such feelings are many and complex, e.g., social conditioning, trauma, mental illness, etc., but ultimately represent a grave delusion. To act on them would signify a kind of revolt against the wise and God-given order of creation. Remedy may therefore be sought in counseling and other licit means that help accept and live the truth of our God-given sex as expressed in our natural body.

Should the various movements of "sexual identity" innovation therefore be opposed?

Yes. Any initiatives that assist or encourage men to "identify" as women or vice versa by chemicals, surgery, attire, or simple assertion — or that claim the civil authority has a right or duty to act as if this were possible or legitimate — must all be firmly rejected and consistently opposed at all levels of society.

What do all such movements have in common?

A brazen rebellion against reality and God's wise, creating will — a rejection of nature and nature's God, who has ordained the biological sex of each person and ordered it to complementarity and procreation. As such, these movements beget widespread confusion about reality itself, and pose a grave threat to the civil order of nations and the salvation of souls.

May a man ever kill legitimately, without being guilty of the sin of murder?

Yes. Through his own voluntary actions, an individual may waive his right to life when: 1. The common good of *social order* is justly enforced by lawful authorities, as in the execution of criminals; 2. *Legitimate defense* is undertaken, as in just warfare or self-defense.

When does society have the right to inflict the death penalty?

The lawfully constituted public authority may put proven criminals to death for the most serious crimes when this is necessary to maintain social order in repairing injustice, protecting the innocent, deterring further crime, and summoning the criminal to true repentance and atonement.

What are the chief exterior sins against chastity?

1. *Fornication*, sexual relations between the unmarried; 2. *Adultery*, sexual relations when one or both parties are married to someone else; 3. *Prostitution*, the sale of sexual acts as a commodity; 4. *Concubinage* or *cohabitation*, the quasi-regular arrangement of sexual intimacy among the unmarried; 5. *Rape*, the forced sexual violation of another; 6. *Pornography*, the creation, distribution, or use of materials designed to arouse lust; 7. Sexual acts *contrary to the natural order*, including: *Contraception*, any deliberate frustration of fertility in the conjugal act; *Sodomy*, sexual relations between persons of the same sex, also called homosexual or lesbian (between women) acts; *Masturbation*, erotic stimulation of one's own genital organs for sexual self-gratification; *Pederasty*, sexual relations between an adult man and a pubescent or adolescent boy; *Pedophilia*, sexual relations between an adult and a child

(either boy or girl); *Bestiality*, sexual relations between a human being and an animal.

What of Catholics who are publicly known to commit such sins?

Catholics engaged in open adultery, cohabitation, pornography, homosexual lifestyle, or political activism for such causes (e.g., the so-called "LGBTQ+ agenda") must be regarded as public sinners, and until they have repented and been reconciled to the Church, they must be denied Holy Communion by any minister of the sacrament (see Mt 18:17).[169]

Does man have a right to property?

Yes. The right to acquire, possess, and use things (also called *ownership*) is inscribed in nature and confirmed by revelation, and was maintained in the civil laws of all nations prior to the twentieth century.

Are political systems that deny the right to private property evil in themselves?

Yes. Be it named *socialism*, *communism*, or otherwise, any system that denies the basic right to property "is in opposition both to reason and to divine revelation"[170] and "intrinsically perverse."[171]

---

[169] See *Code of Canon Law*, can. 915.
[170] Pope Pius XI, Encyclical *Divini Redemptoris* (March 19, 1937), 14.
[171] Pope Pius XI, *Divini Redemptoris*, 58.

Where do such systems exist today?

Spreading first from the communist regime of the Soviet Union in 1917, several countries now employ socialist and neo-Marxist models of government.

What emerging geopolitical movements are especially opposed to subsidiarity?

1. *Globalism*, which advocates for open borders and the dissolution of individual states; 2. *Technocracy*, which would subjugate private rights and liberties through socioeconomic systems entirely dependent on technological gateways controlled by a small number.

What does the eighth commandment require?

It requires perfect respect for the truth. It directly forbids all lying, and indirectly forbids anything that could unjustly injure our neighbor's reputation or honor.

What is a lie?

An expression or outward sign by which we convey something contrary to what we think is true, for the purpose of deceiving our neighbor.

May we ever tell a lie to defend our life, property, or some other good?

No. This is the error of *consequentialism*. We may never "do evil so that good may come" (Rom 3:8). However, we may "hide the truth prudently"[172] for a just cause, as in the use of mental reservation or equivocation.

---

[172] See ST II-II, q. 110, a. 3, rep. 4.

Have sins against this commandment become very widespread in our time?

Yes. Especially following the Second World War, the use of media to distort facts, sway public opinion, and impose false perceptions of reality (e.g., propaganda) has ensnared many in habitual sins against this commandment.

Errors about the Liturgy

How has the Church properly defined the term *liturgy*?

"The sacred liturgy is … the public worship which our Redeemer as Head of the Church renders to the Father, as well as the worship which the community of the faithful renders to its Founder, and through Him to the heavenly Father. It is, in short, the worship rendered by the Mystical Body of Christ in the entirety of its Head and members."[173]

Do the liturgical ceremonies and rubrics also have a spiritual meaning?

Yes. "Every ceremony of the Holy Mass, however small or minimal, contains in itself a positive work, a real meaning, a distinct beauty. They are like the flowers of the field, which, if they are small compared to the sublime cedars, yet in their smallness and beauty they manifest the omnipotence and wisdom of the Creator."[174] For this reason, St. Teresa of Ávila declared: "I would rather die a thousand times than violate the least ceremony of the Church."[175]

---

[173] Pope Pius XII, Encyclical *Mediator Dei*, 20.
[174] Giuseppe Maria Leone, *La vita interiore del sacerdote, modellata sulla vita di Gesù Cristo: Conferenze*, vol. 2 (Valle di Pompei: 1894), 208.
[175] *Life*, chap. 33.

Is the liturgy primarily for the instruction or edification of man?

No. The liturgy is primarily for the glorification of God. In a connected but secondary way, it is also a source of instruction and sanctification for those who participate in it.[176]

May the Catholic hierarchy create novel liturgical forms at will?

No. Liturgical continuity is an essential aspect of the Church's holiness and catholicity: "For our canons and our forms were not given to the churches at the present day, but were wisely and safely transmitted to us from our forefathers."[177]

Isn't any form of worship inherently sacred?

No. Only *traditional* rites enjoy this inherent sanctity—liturgical forms that have been received from antiquity and developed organically in the Church as one body, i.e., in accord with the authentic *sensus fidelium* and the *perennis sensus ecclesiae* (perennial sense of the Church), duly confirmed by the hierarchy.[178]

Why is this link to antiquity so essential for the sanctity of right worship?

God has revealed how He desires to be worshipped: therefore, this sanctity cannot be fabricated or decreed; it can only be humbly received, diligently protected, and reverently handed on. This is

---

[176] See Council of Trent, Session 22, *Decree on the Sacrifice of the Mass*, chap. 1.
[177] St. Athanasius, *Litt. Encycl.*, no. 1.
[178] As affirmed in the Tridentine *Profession of Faith* (1565): "I also receive and admit the accepted and approved ceremonies of the Catholic Church in the solemn administration of the aforesaid sacraments."

the guiding apostolic principle: *Tradidi quod accepi*, "I handed over to you, what I first received" (1 Cor 15:3*). "So then, brethren, stand firm and hold to the traditions which you were taught by us, either by word of mouth or by letter" (2 Thes 2:15).

Is it possible for a pope or bishop to issue a deficient liturgical form?

Yes. The disciplinary acts of the hierarchy are not infallible; and although such errors are historically rare, even a pope may promulgate a deficient liturgical form, as with the novel Breviary of Pope Paul III (1536)[179] that caused decades of controversy before being retracted by Pope Pius V in 1568.

Is the pope obliged to faithfully maintain the Church's traditional liturgical rites?

Yes. The early medieval Papal Oath affirms: "I promise to keep inviolate the discipline and the liturgy of the Church as I have found them and as they were transmitted by my holy Predecessors,"[180] and the Papal Oath decreed by the Council of Constance echoes: "I will follow and observe in every way the rite handed down of the ecclesiastical sacraments of the Catholic Church."[181]

Have attempts at liturgical innovation ever been condemned by the Church?

Yes. The Jansenist Synod of Pistoia (1786) sought to reduce the liturgy "'to a greater simplicity of rites, by expressing it in the vernacular

---

[179] Also called the "Breviary of Cardinal Quignonez."
[180] *Liber Diurnus Romanorum Pontificum*. This oath was in use from the eighth through the tenth century.
[181] Session 39 (October 9, 1417), ratified by Pope Martin V.

language, by uttering it in a loud voice'; as if the present order of the liturgy, received and approved by the Church, had emanated in some part from the forgetfulness of the principles by which it should be regulated"—a notion condemned as "rash, offensive to pious ears, insulting to the Church, favorable to the charges of heretics against it."[182] Pope Benedict XVI similarly affirmed: "In the history of the liturgy there is growth and progress, but no rupture. What earlier generations held as sacred, remains sacred and great for us too, and it cannot be all of a sudden entirely forbidden or even considered harmful."[183]

Why is the Latin language so well suited to liturgical prayer?
Because of its: 1. *Sacrality*—removal from profane use reinforces the unique and sacred character of the liturgy; 2. *Antiquity*—emphasizing the unity and perpetuity of the Faith itself; 3. *Stability*—as a "dead" language, its fixed terms and meanings protect the liturgy from doctrinal corruption; 4. *Universality*—expressing and facilitating the unity of the Church's liturgical prayer worldwide.

Can a pope abrogate a liturgical rite of immemorial custom in the Church?
No. Just as a pope cannot forbid or abrogate the Apostles' Creed or Niceno-Constantinopolitan Creed or substitute a new formula for them, neither can he abrogate traditional, millennium-old rites of Mass and the sacraments or forbid their use. This applies as much to Eastern as to Western rites.

---

[182] Pope Pius VI, Apostolic Constitution *Auctorem Fidei* (August 28, 1794), prop. 33.
[183] Letter to the Bishops Accompanying "Summorum Pontificum."

Could the traditional Roman Rite ever be legitimately forbidden for the entire Church?

No. It rests upon divine, apostolic, and ancient pontifical usage, and bears the canonical force of immemorial custom; it can never be abrogated or forbidden.[184]

Doesn't the traditional Roman Rite hinder the Church's unity or evangelizing mission?

No. The Church condemns such notions,[185] and they contradict the facts of history: traditional worship has always fostered the true unity of the Church, and many souls have been drawn to faith precisely by witnessing the doctrinal and ritual integrity, clarity, and beauty of her constant liturgical rites.

Isn't this Rite "clericalist" for excluding laity from the sanctuary during Mass?

No. True participation in the sacred liturgy does not require one's action as a minister. The laity in the nave have the right and duty to interiorly unite themselves to the offering of the Son of God to His Father at the hands of the priest; but in the manner proper to them, without the confusion or symbolic contradiction of their presence in the sanctuary among the ordained ministers. The laity's proper role is to be inwardly sanctified by the sacraments, and to bring all secular matters into subjection to the Kingship of Christ.

---

[184] See Council of Trent, Session 22 (September 17, 1562), and Pope St. Pius V, Bull *Quo Primum* (July 14, 1570). See also Pope Benedict XVI, Motu Proprio *Summorum Pontificum* (July 7, 2007), art. 1.

[185] See Pope Pius VI, *Auctorem Fidei*, prop. 78; Pope Gregory XVI, Encyclical *Quo Graviora* (October 4, 1833), 4.

Isn't this Rite "obscurantist" with its clerical roles, silence, and mysterious elements?

No. All traditional liturgical rites assign varied roles, words, and actions as an image of the many-layered cosmos, visible and invisible, and of the heavenly hierarchies of angels and saints, with Christ at their head. The sacred mysteries, before which saints and angels cover their faces (see Job 40:4; Is 6:2; Apoc 7:11; and 8:1), are appropriately veiled behind a visual or sonic iconostasis or "holy screen," as part of the proper reverence God has commanded (see Ex 33:18–23; 2 Cor 3:7–11).

PART IV

THE BLESSED VIRGIN MARY, DESTROYER OF HERESIES

Devotion to Mary, Destroyer of Heresies

"Rejoice, O Virgin Mary, for thou alone have destroyed all heresies in the whole world. Thou believed the word of the Archangel Gabriel. A virgin still, thou brought forth the God-man; thou bore a Child, O Virgin, and remained a Virgin still. Mother of God, intercede for us." Holy Mother Church has prayed these words for more than a millennium in the Roman Rite, in the Divine Office and Mass of the Blessed Virgin Mary.[186]

The battle of the Blessed Virgin Mary against Satan (the one chiefly responsible for spreading errors and heresies in the world) is already indicated by God's words after the sinful Fall of Adam and Eve: "I will put enmity between you and the Woman, between your offspring and hers. He will crush your head while you will strike at his heel" (Gen 3:15). In his Marian Encyclical *Redemptoris Mater*, Pope John Paul II taught that Mary is collocated in the very center of the battle of Christ against Satan: "Mary, Mother of the Incarnate Word, is placed at the very center of that enmity, that struggle which accompanies the history of humanity on earth

---

[186] Tract after Septuagesima, from the Common of the Blessed Virgin Mary.

and the history of salvation itself. In this history Mary remains a sign of sure hope."[187]

Why has the Blessed Virgin Mary "destroyed all heresies," when we continue to see errors throughout the world? Because she was the first to hold explicit faith in the historical incarnation of the Son of God, the essential grounding of the Christian faith; for, the one who believes in the true divinity of Christ will accept all that Christ teaches, and order his life accordingly. As the first to fully embrace this living faith in the Incarnation of God, the Blessed Virgin Mary is herself a perpetual vessel and testament of that Faith on earth—a Faith which will never perish, but will endure until the Last Judgment. Through the faith and fidelity of Mary, the true Faith was established on earth, and she who was first to believe is therefore most powerful to destroy all unbelief and heresy.

For this reason, Pope Pius X (+1914) spoke about Our Lady as the noblest foundation of the house of our faith:

> To Mary it was said: "Blessed is she who has believed, because the things promised Her by the Lord shall be accomplished" (Lk 1:45). The promise was that she would conceive and bring forth the Son of God.... Therefore, since the Son of God made Man is the "author and finisher of faith" (Heb 12:2), we must recognize His most holy Mother as the partaker and, as it were, the custodian, of the divine mysteries. We must acknowledge that, after Christ, she is the noblest foundation on which is built the house of faith for all ages.[188]

---

[187] 11.

[188] Encyclical *Ad Diem Illum* (February 2, 1904), 5.

The same pope continues to explain the dogma of the Immaculate Conception of the Blessed Virgin as the most powerful bulwark against modern unbelief, and further illuminates the title of Mary as Destroyer of All Heresies:

> What truly is the point of departure of the enemies of religion for the sowing of the great and serious errors by which the faith of so many is shaken? They begin by denying that man has fallen by sin and been cast down from his former position. Hence, they regard as mere fables original sin and the evils that were its consequence. Humanity, vitiated in its source, vitiated in its turn the whole race of man; and thus was evil introduced amongst men and the necessity for a Redeemer involved. All this rejected, it is easy to understand that no place is left for Christ, for the Church, for grace, or for anything that is above and beyond nature; in one word the whole edifice of faith is shaken from top to bottom. But let people believe and confess that the Virgin Mary has been from the first moment of her conception preserved from all stain; and it is straightway necessary that they should admit both original sin and the rehabilitation of the human race by Jesus Christ, the Gospel, the Church, and the law of suffering. By virtue of this, Rationalism and Materialism are torn up by the roots and destroyed, and there remains to Christian wisdom the glory of having to guard and protect the truth. It is moreover a vice common to the enemies of the faith of our time especially that they repudiate and proclaim the necessity of repudiating all respect and obedience for the authority of the Church,

and even of any human power, in the idea that it will thus be more easy to make an end of faith. Here we have the origin of Anarchism, than which nothing is more pernicious and pestilent to the order of things, whether natural or supernatural. Now this plague, which is equally fatal to society at large and to Christianity, finds its ruin in the dogma of the Immaculate Conception—by the obligation which it imposes of recognizing in the Church a power before which not only the will must bow, but the intelligence must subject itself. It is from this sort of subjection of the reason that Christian people sing thus the praise of the Mother of God: "Thou art all fair, O Mary, and the stain of original sin is not in thee" (Mass of the Immaculate Conception). And thus, once again is justified what the Church attributes to this august Virgin: that she has exterminated all heresies in the world.[189]

In the year 1602, after Saint Francis de Sales (+1622) successfully crushed Protestantism in the region of Chablais after long and hard work and preaching, he wrote on the arch of the choir of the church in Thonon, the principal town of that region, the words: *Gaude Maria virgo, cunctas haereses sola interemisti in universo mundo* (Rejoice, O Virgin Mary, for thou alone have destroyed all heresies in the whole world). Thus did this Saint and Doctor of the Church confess, in a solemn way, the Blessed Virgin Mary as the guardian of the fundaments of the whole Christian life, of the true Faith.

Saint Louis Grignion de Monfort (+1716) says, in his *Treatise on True Devotion to the Blessed Virgin*:

---

[189] Ibid., 22.

Mary has authority over the angels and the blessed in heaven. As a reward for her great humility, God gave her the power and the mission of assigning to saints the thrones made vacant by the apostate angels who fell away through pride. Such is the will of almighty God who exalts the humble, that the powers of heaven, earth, and hell, willingly or unwillingly, must obey the commands of the humble Virgin Mary. For God has made her queen of heaven and earth, leader of his armies, keeper of his treasures, dispenser of his graces, worker of his wonders, restorer of the human race, mediatrix on behalf of men, destroyer of his enemies, and faithful associate in his great works and triumphs.... Satan fears her not only more than all Angels and men, but in some sense more than God Himself... because Satan, being proud, suffers infinitely more from being beaten and punished by a little and humble handmaid of God, and her humility humbles him more than the Divine power.[190]

The Venerable Mother Maria of Agreda (+1665), who lived in Spain in the seventeenth century, recorded several profound insights into the faith of the Blessed Virgin Mary and its connection to our own faith. A number of passages from her renowned work *The Mystical City of God* are worth careful consideration:

> In few words the holy Elizabeth described the greatness of the faith of most holy Mary, when, as reported to us by the evangelist Luke, She exclaimed: "Blessed art thou

[190] 28, 52.

for having believed, because the words and promises of the Lord shall be fulfilled in Thee" (Luke 1, 45)....

The faith of the most holy Mary was an image of the whole creation and an open prodigy of the divine power, for in Her the virtue of faith existed in the highest and the most perfect degree possible; in a certain manner and to a great extent, it made up for the want of faith in men. The Most High has given this excellent virtue to mortals so that, in spite of the carnal and mortal nature, they might have the knowledge of the Divinity and of his mysteries and admirable works: a knowledge so certain and infallibly secure, that it is like seeing Him face to face, and like the vision of the blessed angels in heaven. The same object and the same truth, which they see openly, we perceive obscured under the veil of faith.

One glance at the world will make us understand, how many nations, reigns and provinces, since the beginning of the world, have lost their claims to this great blessing of the faith, so little understood by the thankless mortals: how many have unhappily flung it aside, after the Lord had conferred it on them in his generous mercy, and how many of the faithful, having without their merit received the gift of faith, neglect and despise it, letting it lie idle and unproductive for the last end to which it is to direct and guide them. It was befitting therefore, that the divine equity should have some recompense for such lamentable loss, and that such an incomparable benefit should find an adequate and proportionate return, as far as is possible from creatures; it was befitting that there should be found at least one Creature, in whom the virtue of faith should come to its fullest perfection, as an example and rule for the rest.

All this was found in the great faith of the most holy Mary and on account of Her and for Her alone, if there had been no other creature in the world, it would have been most proper, that God should contrive and create the excellent virtue of faith; for according to our way of understanding, Mary by Herself was a sufficient pledge to the divine Providence, that He would find a proper return on the part of man, and that the object of this faith would not be frustrated by the want of correspondence among mortals. The faith of this sovereign Queen was to make recompense for their default and She was to copy the divine prototype of this virtue in its highest perfection. All the other faithful can measure and gauge themselves by the faith of this Mistress; for they will be more or less faithful, the more or less they approach the perfection of her incomparable faith. Therefore She was set as Teacher and example of all the believing, including the Patriarchs, Prophets, Apostles and Martyrs and all that have believed or will believe in the Christian doctrines to the end of the world.

… Our supereminent Lady, Mary, possesses much greater rights and titles to be called the Mother of faith and of all the faithful. In Her hand is hoisted the standard and ensign of faith for all the believers in the law of grace. First indeed, according to the order of time, was the Patriarch [Abraham]; and consequently he was ordained to be the father and head of the Hebrew people: great was his belief in the promises concerning Christ our Lord and in the works of the Most High. Nevertheless, incomparably more admirable was the faith of Mary in all these regards and She excels him in dignity. Greater difficulty and incongruity was there that a virgin should conceive and bring forth, than that an aged and sterile woman should bear fruit; and the patriarch Abraham was not so certain of the sacrifice of Isaac, as Mary was of the inevitable sacrifice of her most holy Son. She is the One, who perfectly believed and hoped in all the mysteries, and She shows to the whole Church, how it must believe in the Most High and in the works of his Redemption. Having thus understood the faith of Mary our Queen, we must admit Her to be the Mother of the faithful and the prototype of the Catholic faith and of holy hope....

The inestimable treasure of the virtue of divine faith is hidden to those mortals who have only carnal and earthly eyes; for they do not know how to appreciate and esteem a gift and blessing of such incomparable value. Consider ... what the world was without faith and what it would be today if ... [the] Lord would not preserve faith. How many men whom the world has celebrated as great, powerful, and wise have precipitated themselves, on account of the want of light of faith, from the darkness of their unbelief into most abominable sins, and thence into the eternal darkness of hell!... And they are followed by the bad Christians, who having received the grace and blessing of faith, live as if they had it not in their hearts.[191]

Venerable Mary of Agreda thus reminds us to be most grateful for the "precious jewel" of faith which the Lord has given, and to strive continually to exercise this virtue which brings the soul ever closer to heaven, the ultimate object of all our desires. She continues:

> Faith teaches the sure way of eternal salvation, faith is the light that shines in the darkness of this mortal life and pilgrimage; it leads men securely to the possession of the fatherland to which they are wayfaring, if they do not allow it to die out by infidelity and sinfulness. Faith enlivens the other virtues and serves as a nourishment of the just man and a support in his labors. Faith confounds and fills with fear the infidels and the lax Christians in their negligence; for it convinces them in this world of their sin and threatens punishment in the life to come. Faith is powerful to do all things, for nothing is impossible to the believer; faith makes all things attainable and possible. Faith illumines and ennobles the understanding of man, since it directs him in the darkness of his natural ignorance, not to stray from the way, and it elevates him above himself so that he sees and understands with infallible certainty what is far above his powers and assures him of it no less than if he saw it clearly before him. He is thus freed from the gross and vile narrow-mindedness of those who will believe only

[191] Book 2, chap. 6.

what they can experience by their own limited natural powers, not considering that the soul, as long as it lives in the prison of this corruptible body, is very much circumscribed and limited in its sphere of action by the knowledge drawn from the coarse activity of the senses. [Let us] appreciate, therefore ... this priceless treasure of the Catholic faith given ... by God, watch over it and practice it in great esteem and reverence.[192]

The outstanding saint and martyr of the twentieth century, St. Maximilian Kolbe (+1941), first conceived of the idea of founding his worldwide Marian apostolate the *Militia Immaculatae* ("Militia of the Immaculata") in the context of an outrageous public demonstration against the Faith in 1917:

> Freemasons in Rome began to demonstrate openly and belligerently against the Church. They placed the black standard of the "Giordano Bruno" under the window of the Vatican. On this standard the archangel St. Michael was depicted lying under the feet of the triumphant Lucifer. At the same time, countless pamphlets were distributed to the people in which the Holy Father was attacked shamefully. Right then I conceived the idea of organizing an active society to counteract Freemasonry and other slaves of Lucifer.[193]

---

[192] Ibid.
[193] "How the Militia of the Immaculata Began," *Immaculata* (Jan–Feb, 1999), 16: first published in the November 1935 issue of the *Mugenzai no Seibo no Kishi*, the Japanese edition of the *Immaculata* magazine, commemorating the eighteenth anniversary of the Militia Immaculata.

St. Maximilian Kolbe would further describe these Masonic demonstrations in the 1939 issue of his magazine, *Miles Immaculatae*:

> Enraged hands dared to write such slogans as, "Satan will rule on Vatican Hill, and the Pope will serve as his lackey," and other such insults. Now these unreasoning acts of hatred toward the Church of Christ and his temporal Vicar were not the inept rantings of a few individual psychopaths, but the manner, way and plan of action deduced from the Masonic rule: Destroy all teaching about God, especially the Catholic teaching.... In their plan they use many and various kinds of societies, which under their leadership promote neglect of Divine things and the breakdown of morality. This is because the Freemasons follow this principle above all: "Catholicism can be overcome not by logical arguments but by corrupted morals." And so, they overwhelm the souls of men with the kind of literature and arts that will most easily destroy a sense of chaste morals, and foster sordid lifestyles in all phases of human life.... To bring help to so many unhappy persons, to stabilize innocent hearts so that all can more easily go to the Immaculate Virgin through whom so many graces come down to us, the *Militia Immaculatae* was established in Rome in 1917.[194]

---

[194] Originally published in *Miles Immaculatae* (July–Sep, 1939), No. 3 (7), 66–72: trans. Fr. Bernard M. Geiger, OFM Conv in the unpublished work, *The MI in the Words of Its Founder, Vol. I: Selections from the Writings of St. Maximilian Maria Kolbe on the* Militia Immaculatae, *the Blessed Virgin Mary, and the General Topic of How One Lives the Life of an MI* (Conventual Franciscan Friars of Marytown: Libertyville, undated), 8–9.

If St. Maximilian Kolbe were a priest on earth today, one can only imagine what he would think of the graphic immorality now produced or promoted by media outlets everywhere—whether in news or entertainment, through radio, television, personal technologies, and more—and to what extent Freemasonry continues to be responsible for the same. Even so, we are confident that the humble and immaculate Virgin Mary will always crush the proud head of Satan (see Gen 3:15), and that she will surely crush the great heresy of all times, which is the *heresy of the Anti-Christ*.

HERESY OF THE ANTI-CHRIST

"Who is a liar, but he who denieth that Jesus is the Christ? This is Antichrist, who denieth the Father, and the Son" (1 Jn 2:22). The greatest enemy of the Christian faith is not an army with material weapons, but an army of those who are equipped with ink and pen in order to undermine and pervert the virginal purity of the Catholic faith.

In his *The Ballad of the White Horse* (a great poetic meditation on the English King Alfred the Great's defeat of the heathen King of Denmark in 878), the celebrated Catholic author G. K. Chesterton (+1936) puts the following words in the mouth of King Alfred, relating a vision after his victory over the pagan army:

> ...Though they scatter now and go,
> In some far century, sad and slow,
> I have a vision, and I know
> The heathen shall return.
> They shall not come with warships,
> They shall not waste with brands,
> But books be all their eating,

And ink be on their hands....
Not with the humour of hunters
Or savage skill in war,
But ordering all things with dead words,...
What though they come with scroll and pen,
And grave as a shaven clerk,
By this sign you shall know them,
That they ruin and make dark;...
By God and man dishonoured,
By death and life made vain,
Know ye the old barbarian,
The barbarian come again.

We certainly witness this return to heathenism in our time, in the explosion of gender ideology in all its forms — from feminism to "LGBTQ+" movements, transgenderism, and legal recognition of all manner of so-called "unions" as on a par with true marriage. The common threads connecting these phenomena are the spirit of Anti-Christ — denial of the Son of God come in the flesh — and an accompanying spirit of Anti-Mary — the rejection of our own human nature, and refusal to submit to the Incarnate Son of God in that same nature. Contrary to the Blessed Virgin's *Magnificat* (see Lk 1:46–55) proclaiming the greatness of God realized in her own body and soul, the spirit of Anti-Mary tends to a kind of atheistic androgyny: scorning the divine gift of human embodiment, viewing God's design of the naturally complementary sexes as merely dispensable social constructs, and using the human body itself as a dispensable external apparatus, to be manipulated at will.

This tendency is further evident in calls for the sacramental ordination of women in the Catholic Church. Despite the ontological impossibility of such an ordination, all advocacy for it not only signifies a rejection of the divine constitution of holy orders, but also of femininity itself, exemplified above all in Our Lady. For, despite being most worthy for such a service, there is no record of the Blessed Virgin Mary ever performing any liturgical function in the primitive Church. As recalled by St. Epiphanius:

> If it were ordained by God that women should offer sacrifice or have any canonical function in the Church, Mary herself, if anyone, should have functioned as a priest in the New Testament.... But it was not God's pleasure [that she be a priest]. She was not even entrusted with the administration of baptism — for Christ could have been baptized by her rather than by John.[195]

Our Lady avoided all this, simply by acknowledging God's wise and provident designs in both nature and grace. Every minister of the sacraments in the Church represents Christ, signifying degrees of His service, priesthood, and headship, and their various services are therefore performed by ordained men — or, in their absence, by their deputies: male readers and altar servers. For this reason, the Church even forbids artistic works that could give the impression of Our Lady being a priest.[196] Indeed, "Marian participation" in the liturgy — one of intense charity and interior union with Christ — is the most active and fruitful liturgical participation possible for the common priesthood, and especially of women.

---

[195] *Panarion*, bk. 3, Anacephalaeosis VII, sect 79, no. 3.
[196] See *Acta Apostolicae Sedis* 8, yr. 1916, p. 146.

REFUGE AND STRENGTH IN MARY

According to St. Louis Grignion de Montfort, Our Lady needs new apostles in order to prepare, with Her, the triumph and final victory of Jesus. These apostolic souls should be instructed by Mary and totally consecrated to her service, entirely dedicated in her hands to the mission of snatching souls from the darkness of errors, and from danger of the final perdition — as we witness in our days a growing immensity of evil, which the powers of darkness seem to have installed in all corners of the world.

In St. Louis Grignion de Monfort's preaching of the gospel and spiritual teachings, it may seem scandalous or harsh to read his language insisting on *Marian slavery*, with the notion of belonging entirely to the Virgin Mother of God. Yet, we are living in a world of slavery: the slavery of money, of power, of lust, of the passions, of the fashions, of public opinion, of narcotics, television, internet, pornography, and more. The results are before our eyes: despair, frustration, neurosis, violence, degradation — the very "wages of sin," according to the words of St. Paul (cf. Rom 6:23).

The original temptation, "You shall be as God" (Gn 3:5), now drives men to all kinds of slavery under the pretext of freedom. The cry: "It's forbidden to forbid!" has opened the door to unspeakable violence and depravations, both of soul and body. By contrast, the chains which bind one to Mary as her servant and slave are really *wings*, according to St. Louis Grignion de Monfort. Just as Jesus came to us through Mary, so let us go back to Him along the same wonderful way that He came to us — this is the opening invitation and summary of St. Louis Grignion de Monfort's entire spiritual program of "Total Consecration," a sacred Code of Catholic spirituality for the end-times, capable of forming apostles, saints, and combatants for the last battles which the Apocalypse indicates.

Pope Leo XIII further emphasizes the prayer of the holy Rosary and the veneration of the powerful Queen of the holy Rosary as the surest means of help and protection in times of spiritual danger, increased by the spreading of heresies:

> It has always been the habit of Catholics in danger and in troublous times to fly for refuge to Mary, and to seek for peace in Her maternal goodness; showing that the Catholic Church has always, and with justice, put all her hope and trust in the Mother of God. And truly the Immaculate Virgin, chosen to be the Mother of God and thereby associated with Him in the work of man's salvation, has a favor and power with Her Son greater than any human or angelic creature has ever obtained, or ever can gain. And, as it is Her greatest pleasure to grant Her help and comfort to those who seek Her, it cannot be doubted that She would deign, and even be anxious, to receive the aspirations of the universal Church. This devotion, so great and so confident, to the august Queen of Heaven, has never shone forth with such brilliancy as when the militant Church of God has seemed to be endangered by the violence of heresy spread abroad, or by an intolerable moral corruption, or by the attacks of powerful enemies. Ancient and modern history, and the more sacred annals of the Church, bear witness to public and private supplications addressed to the Mother of God, to the help She has granted in return, and to the peace and tranquility which She had obtained from God. Hence Her

illustrious titles of helper, consoler, mighty in war, victorious, and peace-giver. And amongst these is specially to be commemorated that familiar title derived from the Rosary by which the signal benefits She has gained for the whole of Christendom have been solemnly perpetuated.[197]

Saint Pius X similarly encourages Catholics to take refuge in Our Lady in times of persecution of the Catholic faith:

> We earnestly desire that everyone in the world who is called a Christian will draw near to this love of the Virgin during this time when we honor the Mother of God in a more solemn manner. The persecution of Christ and the most holy religion He founded is now raging bitterly and fiercely. At this present time, therefore, there is a serious danger that many will be deceived by the increasing number of errors and ultimately abandon the Faith. "Therefore, let him who thinks he stands take heed lest he fall" (1 Cor 10:12). More than that, let us all humbly beg God through the intercession of the Mother of God that those who have fallen from the path of truth may repent.... The Church will always be attacked, "for there must be factions, so that those who are approved may be made manifest among you" (1 Cor 11:19). The Virgin, however, will always assist us in even the most difficult trials; She will always continue the battle She has been waging ever since Her conception. Thus, every day we can say: "Today the head of the ancient serpent was

---

[197] Encyclical *Supremi Apostolatus Officio*, September 1, 1883.

crushed by Her" (Antiphon of the Office of the Immaculate Conception).[198]

In the Dogmatic Constitution *Lumen Gentium*, the Second Vatican Council maintained that the Church, "imitating the Mother of her Lord, and by the power of the Holy Spirit, keeps with virginal purity the entire faith."[199] Saint Augustine similarly spoke of the Church as a "chaste virgin whom the Apostle speaks of as espoused to Christ (cf. 2 Cor 11:2)," exhorting all Christians in turn:

> Do, in the inner chambers of your soul, what you view with amazement in the flesh of Mary. He who believes in his heart unto justice conceives Christ; he who with his mouth makes profession of the right faith unto salvation brings forth Christ. Thus, in your souls, let fertility abound and virginity be preserved.[200]

The most dangerous corruption which Satan spreads is a corruption of the mind: the corruption of the virginal purity of Catholic doctrine. The battle between Mary and Satan, between the Church and Satan will last until the end of the time, but Satan will never conquer the purity of the faith of Mary and the integrity of the doctrine of the Church; because there will always remain souls of simplicity and purity, maintaining the invincible *sensus fidelium* ("sense of the faithful") inside the Church. A true child and a true servant of Mary will always keep intact and pure the holy Catholic faith, recognizing that sins against the purity of the Catholic faith signify a slandering of the virginal purity of the Blessed Ever-Virgin

---

[198] Encyclical *Ad Diem Illum*, February 2, 1904.
[199] 64.
[200] *Serm.* 191.

Mary. Furthermore, the virtuous purity of faith is deeply linked with the virtue of chastity. Sins against the purity of faith — e.g., sins of heresy — spoil the soul and cause it to lose that virginal purity of the mind, of the intellect, which often result in (or arise from) a loss of the chaste purity of the body.

Nevertheless, we have reason for hope and confidence. During all the troubles through which the Church has passed in her history, the Blessed Virgin Mary has shown herself the powerful mother of Christians, at the same time instilling fear in all the enemies of the Catholic Faith. Pope Pius XI affirmed:

> Anyone who studies with diligence the records of the Catholic Church will easily recognize that the true patronage of the Virgin Mother of God is linked with all the annals of the Christian name. When, in fact, errors everywhere diffused were bent upon rending the seamless robe of the Church and upon throwing the Catholic world into confusion, our fathers turned with confident soul to her "alone who destroys all heresies in the world" (Roman Breviary), and the victory won through her brought the return of tranquility. ... As in the times of the Crusades, in all Europe there was raised one voice of the people, one supplication; so today, in all the world, the cities, and even the smallest villages, united with courage and strength, with filial and constant insistence, the people seek to obtain from the great Mother of God the defeat of the enemies of Christian and human civilization, to the end that true peace may shine again over tired and erring men. If, then, all will do this with due disposition, with great faith and with fervent piety, it is right to hope that as in the past, so in our day, the Blessed Virgin will obtain from her

divine Son that the waves of the present tempests be calmed and that a brilliant victory crown this rivalry of Christians in prayer.[201]

Therefore, in these our dark times of doctrinal confusion, with its deceitful flashes of relativism, naturalism, and anthropocentrism often masked in terms of "dialogue" or "pastoral accompaniment," let us often invoke our Lady with confidence and filial love: Rejoice, O Virgin Mary, for thou alone have destroyed all heresies in the whole world. Mother of God, pray for us!

| Maria Virgo, cunctas hæreses sola interemisti. Quæ Gabrielis Archangeli dictis credidisti. Dum Virgo Deum et hominem genuisti: et post partum Virgo inviolata permansisti. Dei Genetrix, intercede pro nobis. | Rejoice, O Virgin Mary, for alone thou hast put an end to all heresies. Thou that didst believe the words of the archangel Gabriel. Still a virgin, thou didst bring forth God and man: and after childbirth thou didst remain an inviolate virgin. Mother of God, intercede for us.[202] |

---

[201] Encyclical *Ingravescentibus Malis* (September 29, 1937), 2, 20–21.
[202] Tract, Common Mass of the Blessed Virgin Mary.

APPENDIXES

Syllabus of Errors

Syllabus Errorum, Pope Pius IX

THE RAPID GROWTH OF Liberalism and other intellectual currents in the nineteenth century saw a need for clear magisterial pronouncements, leading to the celebrated 1864 encyclical *Quanta Cura* by Pope Pius IX (+1878). Appearing on the feast of the Immaculate Conception, it was accompanied by an official communication to all bishops of the world, consisting of "A Syllabus containing the most important errors of our time, which have been condemned by our Holy Father Pius IX in Allocutions, at Consistories, in Encyclicals, and other Apostolic Letters." This was the famous *Syllabus Errorum* (Syllabus of Errors), which is fully reproduced in English below.[203]

The Syllabus itself consists entirely of negative propositions, concisely stating various errors that have been condemned by the Church. For better understanding, every statement may therefore be read with the preface: "The Church *rejects* the idea that, etc." Every proposition is footnoted with reference to the magisterial document(s) in which it is officially proscribed.

---

[203] English translation approved by Paul Cardinal Cullen in 1874, see *The Syllabus for the People* (London: Burns and Oates, 1874).

SYLLABUS OF ERRORS

I. Pantheism, Naturalism, and Absolute Rationalism

1. There exists no Supreme, all-wise, all-provident Divine Being, distinct from the universe, and God is identical with the nature of things, and is, therefore, subject to changes. In effect, God is produced in man and in the world, and all things are God and have the very substance of God, and God is one and the same thing with the world, and, therefore, spirit with matter, necessity with liberty, good with evil, justice with injustice.[204]

2. All action of God upon man and the world is to be denied.[205]

3. Human reason, without any reference whatsoever to God, is the sole arbiter of truth and falsehood, and of good and evil; it is law to itself, and suffices, by its natural force, to secure the welfare of men and of nations.[206]

4. All the truths of religion proceed from the innate strength of human reason; hence reason is the ultimate standard by which man can and ought to arrive at the knowledge of all truths of every kind.[207]

5. Divine revelation is imperfect, and therefore subject to a continual and indefinite progress, corresponding with the advancement of human reason.[208]

---

[204] Cf. Allocution *Maxima quidem* (June 9, 1862).
[205] Cf. Allocution *Maxima quidem* (June 9, 1862).
[206] Cf. Allocution *Maxima quidem* (June 9, 1862).
[207] Cf. Encyclical *Qui pluribus* (Nov. 9, 1846); Encyclical *Singulari quidem* (Mar. 17, 1856); Allocution *Maxima quidem* (June 9, 1862).
[208] Cf. Encyclical *Qui pluribus* (Nov. 9, 1846); Allocution *Maxima quidem* (June 9, 1862).

6. The faith of Christ is in opposition to human reason and divine revelation not only is not useful, but is even hurtful to the perfection of man.[209]

7. The prophecies and miracles set forth and recorded in the Sacred Scriptures are the fiction of poets, and the mysteries of the Christian faith the result of philosophical investigations. In the books of the Old and New Testament there are contained mythical inventions, and Jesus Christ is Himself a myth.[210]

II. Moderate Rationalism

8. As human reason is placed on a level with religion itself, so theological must be treated in the same manner as philosophical sciences.[211]

9. All the dogmas of the Christian religion are indiscriminately the object of natural science or philosophy, and human reason, enlightened solely in an historical way, is able, by its own natural strength and principles, to attain to the true science of even the most abstruse dogmas; provided only that such dogmas be proposed to reason itself as its object.[212]

10. As the philosopher is one thing, and philosophy another, so it is the right and duty of the philosopher to subject himself

---

[209] Cf. Encyclical *Qui pluribus* (Nov. 9, 1846); Allocution *Maxima quidem* (June 9, 1862).
[210] Cf. Encyclical *Qui pluribus* (Nov. 9, 1846); Allocution *Maxima quidem* (June 9, 1862).
[211] Cf. Allocution *Singulari quadam* (Dec. 9, 1854).
[212] Cf. Letter *Gravissimas inter* (Dec. 11, 1862); Letter *Tuas libenter* (Dec. 21, 1863).

to the authority which he shall have proved to be true; but philosophy neither can nor ought to submit to any such authority.[213]

11. The Church not only ought never to pass judgment on philosophy, but ought to tolerate the errors of philosophy, leaving it to correct itself.[214]

12. The decrees of the Apostolic See and of the Roman congregations impede the true progress of science.[215]

13. The method and principles by which the old scholastic doctors cultivated theology are no longer suitable to the demands of our times and to the progress of the sciences.[216]

14. Philosophy is to be treated without taking any account of supernatural revelation.[217]

III. Indifferentism, Latitudinarianism

15. Every man is free to embrace and profess that religion which, guided by the light of reason, he shall consider true.[218]

---

[213] Cf. Letter *Gravissimas inter* (Dec. 11, 1862); Letter *Tuas libenter* (Dec. 21, 1863).
[214] Cf. Letter *Gravissimas inter* (Dec. 11, 1862).
[215] Cf. Letter *Tuas libenter* (Dec. 21, 1863).
[216] Cf. Letter *Tuas libenter* (Dec. 21, 1863).
[217] Cf. Letter *Eximiam tuam* (June 15, 1857); Letter *Dolore haud mediocri* (Apr. 30, 1860); Letter *Tuas libenter* (Dec. 21, 1863).
[218] Cf. Condemnation *Multiplices inter* (June 10, 1851); Allocution *Maxima quidem* (June 9, 1862).

16. Man may, in the observance of any religion whatever, find the way of eternal salvation, and arrive at eternal salvation.[219]

17. Good hope at least is to be entertained of the eternal salvation of all those who are not at all in the true Church of Christ.[220]

18. Protestantism is nothing more than another form of the same true Christian religion, in which form it is given to please God equally as in the Catholic Church.[221]

IV. Socialism, Communism, Secret Societies, Biblical Societies, Clerico-Liberal Societies

Pests of this kind are frequently reprobated in the severest terms in the Encyclical *Qui pluribus* (Nov. 9, 1846), Allocution *Quibus quantisque* (April 20, 1849), Encyclical *Nostis et nobiscum* (Dec. 8, 1849), Allocution *Singulari quadam* (Dec. 9, 1854), and Encyclical *Quanto conficiamur moerore* (Aug. 10, 1863).

V. Errors Concerning the Church and Her Rights

19. The Church is not a true and perfect society, entirely free — nor is she endowed with proper and perpetual rights of her own, conferred upon her by her Divine Founder; but it appertains to the civil power to define what are the rights of the Church, and the limits within which she may exercise those rights.[222]

---

[219] Cf. Allocution *Ubi primum* (Dec. 17, 1847); Encyclical *Singulari quidem* (Mar. 17, 1856).
[220] Cf. Allocution *Singulari quadam* (Dec. 9, 1854); Encyclical *Quanto conficiamur moerore* (Aug. 10, 1863).
[221] Cf. Encyclical *Nostis et Nobiscum* (Dec. 8, 1849).
[222] Cf. Allocution *Singulari quadam* (Dec. 9, 1854); Allocution *Novos et ante* (Sept. 28, 1860); Allocution *Maxima quidem* (June 9, 1862).

20. The ecclesiastical power ought not to exercise its authority without the permission and assent of the civil government.[223]

21. The Church has not the power of defining dogmatically that the religion of the Catholic Church is the only true religion.[224]

22. The obligation by which Catholic teachers and authors are strictly bound is confined to those things only which are proposed to universal belief as dogmas of faith by the infallible judgment of the Church.[225]

23. Roman pontiffs and ecumenical councils have wandered outside the limits of their powers, have usurped the rights of princes, and have even erred in defining matters of faith and morals.[226]

24. The Church has not the power of using force, nor has she any temporal power, direct or indirect.[227]

25. Besides the power inherent in the episcopate, other temporal power has been attributed to it by the civil authority granted either explicitly or tacitly, which on that account is revocable by the civil authority whenever it thinks fit.[228]

26. The Church has no innate and legitimate right of acquiring and possessing property.[229]

---

[223] Cf. Allocution *Meminit unusquisque* (Sept. 30, 1861).
[224] Cf. Condemnation *Multiplices inter* (June 10, 1851).
[225] Cf. Letter *Tuas libenter* (Dec. 21, 1863).
[226] Cf. Condemnation *Multiplices inter* (June 10, 1851).
[227] Cf. Condemnation *Ad apostolicae* (Aug. 22, 1851).
[228] Cf. Condemnation *Ad apostolicae* (Aug. 22, 1851).
[229] Cf. Allocution *Nunquam fore* (Dec. 15, 1856); Encyclical *Incredibili* (Sept. 17, 1863).

27. The sacred ministers of the Church and the Roman pontiff are to be absolutely excluded from every charge and dominion over temporal affairs.[230]

28. It is not lawful for bishops to publish even letters Apostolic without the permission of Government.[231]

29. Favors granted by the Roman pontiff ought to be considered null, unless they have been sought for through the civil government.[232]

30. The immunity of the Church and of ecclesiastical persons derived its origin from civil law.[233]

31. The ecclesiastical forum or tribunal for the temporal causes, whether civil or criminal, of clerics, ought by all means to be abolished, even without consulting and against the protest of the Holy See.[234]

32. The personal immunity by which clerics are exonerated from military conscription and service in the army may be abolished without violation either of natural right or equity. Its abolition is called for by civil progress, especially in a society framed on the model of a liberal government.[235]

---

[230] Cf. Allocution *Maxima quidem* (June 9, 1862).
[231] Cf. Allocution *Nunquam fore* (Dec. 15, 1856).
[232] Cf. Allocution *Nunquam fore* (Dec. 15, 1856).
[233] Cf. Condemnation *Multiplices inter* (June 10, 1851).
[234] Cf. Allocution *Acerbissimum* (Sept. 27, 1852); Allocution *Nunquam fore* (Dec. 15, 1856).
[235] Cf. Letter *Singularis Nobisque* (Sept. 29, 1864).

33. It does not appertain exclusively to the power of ecclesiastical jurisdiction by right, proper and innate, to direct the teaching of theological questions.[236]

34. The teaching of those who compare the Sovereign Pontiff to a prince, free and acting in the universal Church, is a doctrine which prevailed in the Middle Ages.[237]

35. There is nothing to prevent the decree of a general council, or the act of all peoples, from transferring the supreme pontificate from the bishop and city of Rome to another bishop and another city.[238]

36. The definition of a national council does not admit of any subsequent discussion, and the civil authority can assume this principle as the basis of its acts.[239]

37. National churches, withdrawn from the authority of the Roman pontiff and altogether separated, can be established.[240]

38. The Roman pontiffs have, by their too arbitrary conduct, contributed to the division of the Church into Eastern and Western.[241]

---

[236] Cf. Letter *Tuas libenter* (Dec. 21, 1863).
[237] Cf. Condemnation *Ad apostolicae* (Aug. 22, 1851).
[238] Cf. Condemnation *Ad apostolicae* (Aug. 22, 1851).
[239] Cf. Condemnation *Ad apostolicae* (Aug. 22, 1851).
[240] Cf. Allocution *Multis gravibusque* (Dec. 17, 1860); Allocution *Iamdudum cernimus* (Mar. 18, 1861).
[241] Cf. Condemnation *Ad apostolicae* (Aug. 22, 1851).

VI. Errors About Civil Society, Considered Both In Itself and In Its Relation To The Church

39. The State, as being the origin and source of all rights, is endowed with a certain right not circumscribed by any limits.[242]

40. The teaching of the Catholic Church is hostile to the well-being and interests of society.[243]

41. The civil government, even when in the hands of an infidel sovereign, has a right to an indirect negative power over religious affairs. It therefore possesses not only the right called that of "exsequatur," but also that of appeal, called "appellatio ab abusu."[244]

42. In the case of conflicting laws enacted by the two powers, the civil law prevails.[245]

43. The secular power has authority to rescind, declare and render null, solemn conventions, commonly called concordats, entered into with the Apostolic See, regarding the use of rights appertaining to ecclesiastical immunity, without the consent of the Apostolic See, and even in spite of its protest.[246]

44. The civil authority may interfere in matters relating to religion, morality, and spiritual government: hence, it can pass judgment on the instructions issued for the guidance of consciences, conformably with their mission, by the pastors of the Church. Further, it has the right to make enactments regarding the

---

[242] Cf. Allocution *Maxima quidem* (June 9, 1862).
[243] Cf. Allocution *Quibus quantisque* (Apr. 20, 1849).
[244] Cf. Condemnation *Ad apostolicae* (Aug. 22, 1851).
[245] Cf. Condemnation *Ad apostolicae* (Aug. 22, 1851).
[246] Cf. Allocution *In consistoriali* (Nov. 1, 1850); Allocution *Multis gravibusque* (Dec. 17, 1860).

administration of the divine sacraments, and the dispositions necessary for receiving them.[247]

45. The entire government of public schools in which the youth of a Christian state is educated, except (to a certain extent) in the case of episcopal seminaries, may and ought to appertain to the civil power, and belong to it so far that no other authority whatsoever shall be recognized as having any right to interfere in the discipline of the schools, the arrangement of the studies, the conferring of degrees, in the choice or approval of the teachers.[248]

46. Moreover, even in ecclesiastical seminaries, the method of studies to be adopted is subject to the civil authority.[249]

47. The best theory of civil society requires that popular schools open to children of every class of the people, and, generally, all public institutes intended for instruction in letters and philosophical sciences and for carrying on the education of youth, should be freed from all ecclesiastical authority, control, and interference, and should be fully subjected to the civil and political power at the pleasure of the rulers, and according to the standard of the prevalent opinions of the age.[250]

48. Catholics may approve of the system of educating youth unconnected with Catholic faith and the power of the Church, and which regards the knowledge of merely natural things, and only, or at least primarily, the ends of earthly social life.[251]

---

[247] Cf. Allocution *Maxima quidem* (June 9, 1862).
[248] Cf. Allocution *In consistoriali* (Nov. 1, 1850); Allocution *Quibus luctuosissimis* (Sept. 5, 1851).
[249] Cf. Allocution *Nunquam fore* (Dec. 15, 1856).
[250] Cf. Letter *Cum non sine* (July 14, 1864).
[251] Cf. Letter *Cum non sine* (July 14, 1864).

49. The civil power may prevent the prelates of the Church and the faithful from communicating freely and mutually with the Roman pontiff.[252]

50. Lay authority possesses of itself the right of presenting bishops, and may require of them to undertake the administration of the diocese before they receive canonical institution, and the Letters Apostolic from the Holy See.[253]

51. And, further, the lay government has the right of deposing bishops from their pastoral functions, and is not bound to obey the Roman pontiff in those things which relate to the institution of bishoprics and the appointment of bishops.[254]

52. Government can, by its own right, alter the age prescribed by the Church for the religious profession of women and men; and may require of all religious orders to admit no person to take solemn vows without its permission.[255]

53. The laws enacted for the protection of religious orders and regarding their rights and duties ought to be abolished; nay, more, civil Government may lend its assistance to all who desire to renounce the obligation which they have undertaken of a religious life, and to break their vows. Government may also suppress the said religious orders, as likewise collegiate churches and simple benefices, even those of advowson and subject their

---

[252] Cf. Allocution *Maxima quidem* (June 9, 1862).
[253] Cf. Allocution *Nunquam fore* (Dec. 15, 1856).
[254] Cf. Condemnation *Multiplices inter* (June 10, 1851); Allocution *Acerbissimum* (Sept. 27, 1852).
[255] Cf. Allocution *Probe memineritis* (Jan. 22, 1855); Allocution *Nunquam fore* (Dec. 15, 1856).

property and revenues to the administration and pleasure of the civil power.[256]

54. Kings and princes are not only exempt from the jurisdiction of the Church, but are superior to the Church in deciding questions of jurisdiction.[257]

55. The Church ought to be separated from the State, and the State from the Church.[258]

VII. Errors Concerning Natural and Christian Ethics

56. Moral laws do not stand in need of the divine sanction, and it is not at all necessary that human laws should be made conformable to the laws of nature and receive their power of binding from God.[259]

57. The science of philosophical things and morals and also civil laws may and ought to keep aloof from divine and ecclesiastical authority.[260]

58. No other forces are to be recognized except those which reside in matter, and all the rectitude and excellence of morality ought to be placed in the accumulation and increase of riches by every possible means, and the gratification of pleasure.[261]

---

[256] Cf. Allocution *Acerbissimum* (Sept. 27, 1852); Allocution *Cum saepe* (July 26, 1855).
[257] Cf. Condemnation *Multiplices inter* (June 10, 1851).
[258] Cf. Allocution *Acerbissimum* (Sept. 27, 1852).
[259] Cf. Allocution *Maxima quidem* (June 9, 1862).
[260] Cf. Allocution *Maxima quidem* (June 9, 1862).
[261] Cf. Allocution *Maxima quidem* (June 9, 1862); Encyclical *Quanto conficiamur moerore* (Aug. 10, 1863).

59. Right consists in the material fact. All human duties are an empty word, and all human facts have the force of right.[262]

60. Authority is nothing else but numbers and the sum total of material forces.[263]

61. The injustice of an act when successful inflicts no injury on the sanctity of right.[264]

62. The principle of non-intervention, as it is called, ought to be proclaimed and observed.[265]

63. It is lawful to refuse obedience to legitimate princes, and even to rebel against them.[266]

64. The violation of any solemn oath, as well as any wicked and flagitious action repugnant to the eternal law, is not only not blamable but is altogether lawful and worthy of the highest praise when done through love of country.[267]

VIII. Errors Concerning Christian Marriage

65. The doctrine that Christ has raised marriage to the dignity of a sacrament cannot be at all tolerated.[268]

---

[262] Cf. Allocution *Maxima quidem* (June 9, 1862).
[263] Cf. Allocution *Maxima quidem* (June 9, 1862).
[264] Cf. Allocution *Iamdudum cernimus* (Mar. 18, 1861).
[265] Cf. Allocution *Novos et ante* (Sept. 28, 1860).
[266] Cf. Encyclical *Qui pluribus* (Nov. 9, 1846); Allocution *Quisque vestrum* (Oct. 4, 1847); Encyclical *Nostis et Nobiscum* (Dec. 8, 1849); Apostolic Letter *Cum catholica Ecclesia* (Mar. 26, 1860).
[267] Cf. Allocution *Quibus quantisque* (Apr. 20, 1849).
[268] Cf. Condemnation *Ad apostolicae* (Aug. 22, 1851).

66. The Sacrament of Marriage is only something accessory to the contract and separate from it, and the sacrament itself consists in the nuptial benediction alone.[269]

67. By the law of nature, the marriage tie is not indissoluble, and in many cases divorce properly so called may be decreed by the civil authority.[270]

68. The Church has not the power of establishing diriment impediments of marriage, but such a power belongs to the civil authority by which existing impediments are to be removed.[271]

69. In the dark ages the Church began to establish diriment impediments, not by her own right, but by using a power borrowed from the State.[272]

70. The canons of the Council of Trent, which anathematize those who dare to deny to the Church the right of establishing diriment impediments, either are not dogmatic or must be understood as referring to such borrowed power.[273]

71. The form of solemnizing marriage prescribed by the Council of Trent, under pain of nullity, does not bind in cases where the civil law lays down another form, and declares that when this new form is used the marriage shall be valid.[274]

---

[269] Cf. Condemnation *Ad apostolicae* (Aug. 22, 1851).
[270] Cf. Condemnation *Ad apostolicae* (Aug. 22, 1851); Allocution *Acerbissimum* (Sept. 27, 1852).
[271] Cf. Condemnation *Multiplices inter* (June 10, 1851).
[272] Cf. Condemnation *Ad apostolicae* (Aug. 22, 1851).
[273] Cf. Condemnation *Ad apostolicae* (Aug. 22, 1851).
[274] Cf. Condemnation *Ad apostolicae* (Aug. 22, 1851).

72. Boniface VIII was the first who declared that the vow of chastity taken at ordination renders marriage void.[275]

73. In force of a merely civil contract there may exist between Christians a real marriage, and it is false to say either that the marriage contract between Christians is always a sacrament, or that there is no contract if the sacrament be excluded.[276]

74. Matrimonial causes and espousals belong by their nature to civil tribunals.[277]

IX. Errors Regarding the Civil Power of the Sovereign Pontiff

75. The children of the Christian and Catholic Church are divided amongst themselves about the compatibility of the temporal with the spiritual power.[278]

76. The abolition of the temporal power of which the Apostolic See is possessed would contribute in the greatest degree to the liberty and prosperity of the Church.[279]

---

[275] Cf. Condemnation *Ad apostolicae* (Aug. 22, 1851).
[276] Cf. Condemnation *Ad apostolicae* (Aug. 22, 1851); Letter to the King of Sardinia (Sept. 9, 1852); Allocution *Acerbissimum* (Sept. 27, 1852); Allocution *Multis gravibusque* (Dec. 17, 1860).
[277] Cf. Condemnation *Ad apostolicae* (Aug. 22, 1851); Allocution *Acerbissimum* (Sept. 27, 1852).
[278] Cf. Condemnation *Ad apostolicae* (Aug. 22, 1851).
[279] Cf. Allocution *Quibus quantisque* (Apr. 20, 1849); Allocution *Si semper antea* (May 20, 1850); Apostolic Letter *Cum catholica Ecclesia* (Mar. 26, 1860); Allocution *Novos et ante* (Sept. 28, 1860); Allocution *Iamdudum cernimus* (Mar. 18, 1861); Allocution *Maxima quidem* (June 9, 1862).

X. Errors Having Reference To Modern Liberalism

77. In the present day it is no longer expedient that the Catholic religion should be held as the only religion of the State, to the exclusion of all other forms of worship.[280]

78. Hence it has been wisely decided by law, in some Catholic countries, that persons coming to reside therein shall enjoy the public exercise of their own peculiar worship.[281]

79. Moreover, it is false that the civil liberty of every form of worship, and the full power, given to all, of overtly and publicly manifesting any opinions whatsoever and thoughts, conduce more easily to corrupt the morals and minds of the people, and to propagate the pest of indifferentism.[282]

80. The Roman Pontiff can, and ought to, reconcile himself, and come to terms with progress, liberalism, and modern civilization.[283]

---

[280] Cf. Allocution *Nemo vestrum* (July 26, 1855).
[281] Cf. Allocution *Acerbissimum* (Sept. 27, 1852).
[282] Cf. Allocution *Nunquam fore* (Dec. 15, 1856).
[283] Cf. Allocution *Iamdudum cernimus* (Mar. 18, 1861).

APPENDIXES

Syllabus Against the Modernists

Lamentabili Sane, Pope Pius X

A generation having passed since the 1864 Syllabus of Pope Pius IX (+1878), the Church faced a new and complex challenge in the heresy of *modernism*, which Pope Pius X (+1914) termed "the synthesis of all heresies." Like the prior Syllabus of 1864, *Lamentabili Sane* was issued on July 3, 1907, to clearly identify certain philosophical and theological errors taking root at the time, and to authoritatively proscribe them as contrary to Catholic faith and morals.[284] Those who adopted or defended any of the ideas listed below were subject to automatic excommunication.

Condemning the errors of the modernists

With truly lamentable results, our age, casting aside all restraint in its search for the ultimate causes of things, frequently pursues novelties so ardently that it rejects the legacy of the human race. Thus it falls into very serious errors, which are even more serious when they concern sacred authority, the interpretation of Sacred Scripture, and the principal mysteries of Faith. The fact that many Catholic writers also go beyond the limits determined by the Fathers and the Church herself is extremely regrettable. In the name of higher knowledge and historical research (they say), they are looking for that progress of dogmas which is, in reality, nothing but the corruption of dogmas.

These errors are being daily spread among the faithful. Lest they captivate the faithful's minds and corrupt the purity of their

---

[284] English translation approved by Bishop Peter Bartholome in 1954, see *All Things in Christ* (Westminster: The Newman Press, 1954).

faith, His Holiness, Pius X, by Divine Providence, Pope, has decided that the chief errors should be noted and condemned by the Office of this Holy Roman and Universal Inquisition.

Therefore, after a very diligent investigation and consultation with the Reverend Consultors, the Most Eminent and Reverend Lord Cardinals, the General Inquisitors in matters of faith and morals have judged the following propositions to be condemned and proscribed. In fact, by this general decree, they are condemned and proscribed.

1. The ecclesiastical law which prescribes that books concerning the Divine Scriptures are subject to previous examination does not apply to critical scholars and students of scientific exegesis of the Old and New Testament.

2. The Church's interpretation of the Sacred Books is by no means to be rejected; nevertheless, it is subject to the more accurate judgment and correction of the exegetes.

3. From the ecclesiastical judgments and censures passed against free and more scientific exegesis, one can conclude that the Faith the Church proposes contradicts history and that Catholic teaching cannot really be reconciled with the true origins of the Christian religion.

4. Even by dogmatic definitions the Church's magisterium cannot determine the genuine sense of the Sacred Scriptures.

5. Since the Deposit of Faith contains only revealed truths, the Church has no right to pass judgment on the assertions of the human sciences.

6. The "Church learning" and the "Church teaching" collaborate in such a way in defining truths that it only remains for the

"Church teaching" to sanction the opinions of the "Church learning."

7. In proscribing errors, the Church cannot demand any internal assent from the faithful by which the judgments she issues are to be embraced.

8. They are free from all blame who treat lightly the condemnations passed by the Sacred Congregation of the Index or by the Roman Congregations.

9. They display excessive simplicity or ignorance who believe that God is really the author of the Sacred Scriptures.

10. The inspiration of the books of the Old Testament consists in this: The Israelite writers handed down religious doctrines under a peculiar aspect which was either little or not at all known to the Gentiles.

11. Divine inspiration does not extend to all of Sacred Scriptures so that it renders its parts, each and every one, free from every error.

12. If he wishes to apply himself usefully to Biblical studies, the exegete must first put aside all preconceived opinions about the supernatural origin of Sacred Scripture and interpret it the same as any other merely human document.

13. The Evangelists themselves, as well as the Christians of the second and third generation, artificially arranged the evangelical parables. In such a way they explained the scanty fruit of the preaching of Christ among the Jews.

14. In many narrations the Evangelists recorded, not so much things that are true, as things which, even though false, they judged to be more profitable for their readers.

15. Until the time the canon was defined and constituted, the Gospels were increased by additions and corrections. Therefore there remained in them only a faint and uncertain trace of the doctrine of Christ.

16. The narrations of John are not properly history, but a mystical contemplation of the Gospel. The discourses contained in his Gospel are theological meditations, lacking historical truth concerning the mystery of salvation.

17. The fourth Gospel exaggerated miracles not only in order that the extraordinary might stand out but also in order that it might become more suitable for showing forth the work and glory of the Word Incarnate.

18. John claims for himself the quality of witness concerning Christ. In reality, however, he is only a distinguished witness of the Christian life, or of the life of Christ in the Church at the close of the first century.

19. Heterodox exegetes have expressed the true sense of the Scriptures more faithfully than Catholic exegetes.

20. Revelation could be nothing else than the consciousness man acquired of his revelation to God.

21. Revelation, constituting the object of the Catholic faith, was not completed with the Apostles.

22. The dogmas the Church holds out as revealed are not truths which have fallen from heaven. They are an interpretation of religious facts which the human mind has acquired by laborious effort.

23. Opposition may, and actually does, exist between the facts narrated in Sacred Scripture and the Church's dogmas which rest on them. Thus the critic may reject as false facts the Church holds as most certain.

24. The exegete who constructs premises from which it follows that dogmas are historically false or doubtful is not to be reproved as long as he does not directly deny the dogmas themselves.

25. The assent of faith ultimately rests on a mass of probabilities.

26. The dogmas of the Faith are to be held only according to their practical sense; that is to say, as preceptive norms of conduct and not as norms of believing.

27. The divinity of Jesus Christ is not proved from the Gospels. It is a dogma which the Christian conscience has derived from the notion of the Messias.

28. While He was exercising His ministry, Jesus did not speak with the object of teaching He was the Messias, nor did His miracles tend to prove it.

29. It is permissible to grant that the Christ of history is far inferior to the Christ Who is the object of faith.

30. In all the evangelical texts the name "Son of God" is equivalent only to that of "Messias." It does not in the least way signify that Christ is the true and natural Son of God.

31. The doctrine concerning Christ taught by Paul, John, and the Councils of Nicea, Ephesus and Chalcedon is not that which Jesus taught but that which the Christian conscience conceived concerning Jesus.

32. It is impossible to reconcile the natural sense of the Gospel texts with the sense taught by our theologians concerning the conscience and the infallible knowledge of Jesus Christ.

33. Everyone who is not led by preconceived opinions can readily see that either Jesus professed an error concerning the immediate Messianic coming or the greater part of His doctrine as contained in the Gospels is destitute of authenticity.

34. The critics can ascribe to Christ a knowledge without limits only on a hypothesis which cannot be historically conceived and which is repugnant to the moral sense. That hypothesis is that Christ as man possessed the knowledge of God and yet was unwilling to communicate the knowledge of a great many things to His disciples and posterity.

35. Christ did not always possess the consciousness of His Messianic dignity.

36. The Resurrection of the Savior is not properly a fact of the historical order. It is a fact of merely the supernatural order (neither demonstrated nor demonstrable) which the Christian conscience gradually derived from other facts.

37. In the beginning, faith in the Resurrection of Christ was not so much in the fact itself of the Resurrection as in the immortal life of Christ with God.

38. The doctrine of the expiatory death of Christ is Pauline and not evangelical.

39. The opinions concerning the origin of the Sacraments which the Fathers of Trent held and which certainly influenced their

dogmatic canons are very different from those which now rightly exist among historians who examine Christianity.

40. The Sacraments have their origin in the fact that the Apostles and their successors, swayed and moved by circumstances and events, interpreted some idea and intention of Christ.

41. The Sacraments are intended merely to recall to man's mind the ever-beneficent presence of the Creator.

42. The Christian community imposed the necessity of Baptism, adopted it as a necessary rite, and added to it the obligation of the Christian profession.

43. The practice of administering Baptism to infants was a disciplinary evolution, which became one of the causes why the Sacrament was divided into two, namely, Baptism and Penance.

44. There is nothing to prove that the rite of the Sacrament of Confirmation was employed by the Apostles. The formal distinction of the two Sacraments of Baptism and Confirmation does not pertain to the history of primitive Christianity.

45. Not everything which Paul narrates concerning the institution of the Eucharist (I Cor. 11:23-25) is to be taken historically.

46. In the primitive Church the concept of the Christian sinner reconciled by the authority of the Church did not exist. Only very slowly did the Church accustom herself to this concept. As a matter of fact, even after Penance was recognized as an institution of the Church, it was not called a Sacrament since it would be held as a disgraceful Sacrament.

47. The words of the Lord, "Receive the Holy Spirit; whose sins you shall forgive, they are forgiven them; and whose sins you

shall retain, they are retained" (John 20:22-23), in no way refer to the Sacrament of Penance, in spite of what it pleased the Fathers of Trent to say.

48. In his Epistle (Ch. 5:14-15) James did not intend to promulgate a Sacrament of Christ but only commend a pious custom. If in this custom he happens to distinguish a means of grace, it is not in that rigorous manner in which it was taken by the theologians who laid down the notion and number of the Sacraments.

49. When the Christian supper gradually assumed the nature of a liturgical action those who customarily presided over the supper acquired the sacerdotal character.

50. The elders who fulfilled the office of watching over the gatherings of the faithful were instituted by the Apostles as priests or bishops to provide for the necessary ordering of the increasing communities and not properly for the perpetuation of the Apostolic mission and power.

51. It is impossible that Matrimony could have become a Sacrament of the new law until later in the Church since it was necessary that a full theological explication of the doctrine of grace and the Sacraments should first take place before Matrimony should be held as a Sacrament.

52. It was far from the mind of Christ to found a Church as a society which would continue on earth for a long course of centuries. On the contrary, in the mind of Christ the kingdom of heaven together with the end of the world was about to come immediately.

53. The organic constitution of the Church is not immutable. Like human society, Christian society is subject to a perpetual evolution.

54. Dogmas, Sacraments, and hierarchy, both their notion and reality, are only interpretations and evolutions of the Christian intelligence which have increased and perfected by an external series of additions the little germ latent in the Gospel.

55. Simon Peter never even suspected that Christ entrusted the primacy in the Church to him.

56. The Roman Church became the head of all the churches, not through the ordinance of Divine Providence, but merely through political conditions.

57. The Church has shown that she is hostile to the progress of the natural and theological sciences.

58. Truth is no more immutable than man himself, since it evolved with him, in him, and through him.

59. Christ did not teach a determined body of doctrine applicable to all times and all men, but rather inaugurated a religious movement adapted or to be adapted to different times and places.

60. Christian Doctrine was originally Judaic. Through successive evolutions it became first Pauline, then Joannine, finally Hellenic and universal.

61. It may be said without paradox that there is no chapter of Scripture, from the first of Genesis to the last of the Apocalypse, which contains a doctrine absolutely identical with that which the Church teaches on the same matter. For the same reason,

therefore, no chapter of Scripture has the same sense for the critic and the theologian.

62. The chief articles of the Apostles' Creed did not have the same sense for the Christians of the first ages as they have for the Christians of our time.

63. The Church shows that she is incapable of effectively maintaining evangelical ethics since she obstinately clings to immutable doctrines which cannot be reconciled with modern progress.

64. Scientific progress demands that the concepts of Christian doctrine concerning God, creation, revelation, the Person of the Incarnate Word, and Redemption be re-adjusted.

65. Modern Catholicism can be reconciled with true science only if it is transformed into a non-dogmatic Christianity; that is to say, into a broad and liberal Protestantism.

The following Thursday, the fourth day of the same month and year, all these matters were accurately reported to our Most Holy Lord, Pope Pius X. His Holiness approved and confirmed the decree of the Most Eminent Fathers and ordered that each and every one of the above-listed propositions be held by all as condemned and proscribed.

APPENDIXES

Oath Against Modernism

Sacrorum Antistitum, Pope Pius X

After *Lamentabili Sane*, faced with the alarming discovery that many Catholic schools and seminaries were propagating Modernist tenets in several countries, the third and final anti-Modernist pronouncement of Pope Pius X (+1914) appeared on September 1, 1910: the Motu Proprio *Sacrorum Antistitum*, which contained the famous Oath Against Modernism.[285] Articulating a solemn rejection of the most prominent errors of Modernism, this Oath remained in force from 1910 to 1967, required of all clergy, pastors, confessors, preachers, religious superiors, and seminary professors.

Oath Formula

I, [Name], firmly embrace and accept all and singly those articles which have been defined, set forth, and declared by the Church's inerrant teaching-authority and especially those heads of doctrines which directly conflict with the errors of this age. And,

I confess that God, the beginning and end of all things, can with certainty be known and proved to be by the natural light of reason from those things which are made, that is, by the visible works of creation, even as a cause may be certainly proved from its effects.

I accept and acknowledge the external arguments of revelation, that is, the divine facts, especially miracles and prophecy, and I also accept the most sure proofs of the divine origin of the Christian religion and hold that they are preeminently adapted to the intelligence of all ages and men and, in particular, of this age.

---

[285] English translation from Volume 8 of the *Tradivox Catholic Catechism Index* (Manchester: Sophia Institute Press, 2022).

And with firm faith, I equally believe that the Church, the guardian and teacher of the revealed word, was directly founded by the real and historical Christ himself, as he dwelt with us, and that she was built upon Peter, the prince of the apostolic hierarchy and his successors forever.

I sincerely receive the teaching of the faith as it has been handed down to us from the apostles and orthodox fathers, and handed down in the same sense and meaning; and furthermore, I utterly reject the heretical fiction of the evolution of dogmas, according to which they change from one meaning to another and a meaning contradictory to that meaning which the Church before had given; and equally do I condemn that entire error according to which philosophical discovery suffices, although the divine deposit was given to Christ's bride and given to be faithfully guarded by her, or according to which it [the teaching] is little by little transformed in meaning by the creations of the human consciousness and man's effort, and brought to perfection in the future by an indefinite progression.

I most surely hold and sincerely declare that faith is not a blind realization of religion drawn out of the darkness of the subconscience, morally enlightened by the influence of the heart and the inflexions of the will, but that it is an honest assent by the intellect given to truth accepted, through hearing of the ear, by which we believe as true those things which have been revealed and confirmed by a personal God, our Creator and Lord, and on the basis of the authority of God, who in the highest sense is trustworthy.

Likewise—and this is equally important—I submit myself reverently and with my whole mind to all the condemnations, declarations, and commands contained in the encyclical *Pascendi* and the decree *Lamentabili*, especially in regard to that which they call the history of dogmas. I also reprobate the error of those who assert that the faith offered by the Church may, by any possibility, conflict with history; and the error that it is not possible to harmonize, in the sense in which they are now understood, the Catholic dogmas with the origins of the Christian religion, which are the more trustworthy.

I condemn and reject the opinions of those who say that the more learned Christians may represent at one and the same time two persons, the one a believer, the other a historian, as if it were possible to hold on as a historian to things which are contradictory to the faith of the believer, or lay down premises according to which it follows that dogmas are either false or dubious, just so they be not openly set aside.

Equally do I reprobate that principle of judging the holy scriptures and interpreting them, which, in defiance of the Church's tradition, the analogy of faith, and the rules of the apostolic see, suits itself to the comments of rationalists, and, scarcely less lawlessly than rashly, accepts textual criticism as the one only and supreme rule.

Further, I reject the theory of those who hold that the teacher in the department of historic theology, as well as the writer on its subjects, must place opinion above the principle of the supernatural origin of Catholic tradition and the promise of divine aid in the preservation of all truth, and further, that the writings of the individual fathers must be explained by the principles of science alone, apart from any sacred authority and by the same free judgment that any profane document is studied or investigated.

Finally, I profess myself most averse to the error of the Modernists who hold that in sacred tradition there is not a divine element; or—what is far worse—who reason in a pantheistic sense, so that nothing is left but the bare and naked historic occurrence like unto other occurrences of history, which are left to men to carry on in subsequent periods by their industry, shrewdness, and genius the teaching begun by Christ and his apostles.

And I do most firmly hold to the faith of the fathers and will continue so to do to the last breath of life, the faith concerning the unfailing charism of the truth which now inheres, has inhered, and will always continue to inhere in the episcopal succession from the apostles; that nothing is to be regarded as better or more opportune which the culture of this age or that age can suggest, and that nothing is at any time to be otherwise believed or otherwise understood as the absolute and immutable truth preached from the beginning by the apostles.

To all these things I promise to hold faithfully, sincerely, and wholly, and I promise to keep them inviolably, never departing from them in teaching or by any words or writings. Thus I promise and swear, so help me God and these holy gospels of God.

APPENDIXES

Declaration of Truths

Catholic Prelature (May 31, 2019)

In the opening of the twenty-first century, with doctrinal ambiguity and errors being widely propagated even by the living officeholders of the Church, a group of Roman Catholic prelates from multiple countries issued a joint "Declaration of Truths" on May 31, 2019. In this open letter of worldwide circulation, forty of the "most common errors in the life of the Church of our time" have been plainly articulated and condemned as contrary to Catholic faith and morals.

Explanatory Note

In our time the Church is experiencing one of the greatest spiritual epidemics, that is, an almost universal doctrinal confusion and disorientation, which is a seriously contagious danger for spiritual health and eternal salvation for many souls. At the same time one has to recognize a widespread lethargy in the exercise of the Magisterium on different levels of the Church's hierarchy in our days. This is largely caused by the non-compliance with the Apostolic duty of all members of the hierarchy — as stated also by the Second Vatican Council — to "vigilantly ward off any errors that threaten the flock" (*Lumen Gentium*, 25).

Our time is characterized by an acute spiritual hunger of the Catholic faithful all over the world for a reaffirmation of those truths that are obfuscated, undermined, and denied by some of the most dangerous errors of our time. The faithful who are suffering this spiritual hunger feel themselves abandoned and thus find themselves in a kind of existential periphery. Such a situation urgently demands a concrete remedy. A public declaration of the truths regarding these errors cannot admit a further deferral. Hence we are mindful of the following timeless words of Pope Saint Gregory the Great: "Our tongue may not be slack to exhort, and having undertaken the office of bishops, our silence may not prove our condemnation at the tribunal of the just Judge.... The people committed to our care abandon God, and we are silent. They live in sin, and we do not stretch out a hand to correct" (*In Ev. hom.* 17:3; 14).

We are aware of our grave responsibility as Catholic bishops according to the admonition of Saint Paul, who teaches that God gave to His Church "shepherds and teachers, to equip the saints for the work of ministry, for building up the body of Christ, until we all attain to the unity of the faith and of the knowledge of the Son of God, to mature manhood, to the measure of the stature of the fullness of Christ, so that we may no longer be children, tossed to and fro by the waves and carried about by every wind of doctrine, by human cunning, by craftiness in deceitful schemes. Rather, speaking the truth in love, we are to grow up in every way into him who is the head, into Christ, from whom the whole body, joined and held together by every joint with which it is equipped, when each part is working properly, makes the body grow so that it builds itself up in love" (Eph 4:12–16).

In the spirit of fraternal charity, we publish this Declaration of truths as a concrete spiritual help, so that bishops, priests, parishes, religious convents, lay faithful associations, and private persons as well might have the opportunity to confess either privately or publicly those truths that in our days are mostly denied or disfigured. The following exhortation of the Apostle Paul should be understood as addressed also to each bishop and lay faithful of our time, "Fight the good fight of the faith. Take hold of the eternal life to which you were called and about which you made the good confession in the presence of many witnesses. I charge you in the presence of God, who gives life to all things, and of Christ Jesus, who in his testimony before Pontius Pilate made the good confession, to keep the commandment unstained and free from reproach until the appearing of our Lord Jesus Christ" (1 Tm 6:12–14).

Before the eyes of the Divine Judge and in his own conscience, each bishop, priest, and lay faithful has the moral duty to give witness unambiguously to those truths that in our days are obfuscated, undermined, and denied. Private and public acts of a declaration of these truths could initiate a movement of a confession of the truth, of its defense, and of reparation for the widespread sins against the Faith, for the sins of hidden and open apostasy from Catholic Faith of a not small number both of the clergy and of the lay people. One has to bear in mind, however, that such a movement will not judge itself according to numbers, but according to the truth, as Saint Gregory of Nazianzus said, amidst the general doctrinal confusion of the Arian crisis, that "God does not delight in numbers" (*Or.* 42:7).

In giving witness to the immutable Catholic Faith, clergy and faithful will remember the truth that "the entire body of the faithful cannot err in matters of belief. They manifest this special property by means of the whole people's supernatural discernment in matters of faith, when from the Bishops down to the last of the lay faithful they show universal agreement in matters of faith and morals" (Second Vatican Council, *Lumen Gentium*, 12).

Saints and great Bishops who lived in times of doctrinal crises may intercede for us and guide us with their teaching, as do the following words of Saint Augustine, with which he addressed Pope Saint Boniface I, "Since the pastoral watch-tower is common to all of us who discharge the office of the episcopate (although you are prominent therein on a loftier height), I do what I can in respect of my small portion of the charge, as the Lord condescends by the aid of your prayers to grant me power" (*Contra ep. Pel.* I, 2).

A common voice of the Shepherds and the faithful through a precise declaration of the truths will be without any doubt an efficient means of a fraternal and filial aid for the Supreme Pontiff in the current extraordinary situation of a general doctrinal confusion and disorientation in the life of the Church.

We make this public Declaration in the spirit of Christian charity, which manifests itself in the care for the spiritual health both of the Shepherds and of the faithful, i.e., of all the members of Christ's Body, which is the Church, while being mindful of the following words of Saint Paul in the First Letter to the Corinthians: "That there might be no division in the body, but the members might be mutually careful one for another. If one member suffers any thing, all the members suffer with it; or if one member is honored, all the members rejoice with it. Now you are the body of Christ, and individually members of it" (1 Cor 12:25–27), and in the Letter to the Romans: "As in one body we have many members, but all the members have not the same office: So we being many, are one body in Christ, and every one members one of another. And having different gifts, according to the grace that is given us, either prophecy, to be used according to the rule of faith; or ministry, in ministering; or he that teaches, in doctrine; he that exhorts, in exhorting; hating that which is evil, cleaving to that which is good. Loving one another with the charity of brotherhood, with honor preventing one another. In carefulness not slothful. In spirit fervent. Serving the Lord" (Rom 12:4–11).

The Cardinals and Bishops who sign this "Declaration of the truths" entrust it to the Immaculate Heart of the Mother of God under the invocation *Salus populi Romani* ("Salvation of the

Roman People"), considering the privileged spiritual meaning which this icon has for the Roman Church. May the entire Catholic Church, under the protection of the Immaculate Virgin and Mother of God, "fight intrepidly the fight of the Faith, persist firmly in the doctrine of the Apostles and proceed safely amidst the storms of the world until she reaches the heavenly city" (Preface of the Mass in honor of the Blessed Virgin Mary, "Salvation of the Roman people").

May 31, 2019
✠ Cardinal Raymond Leo Burke
Patron of the Sovereign Military Order of Malta
✠ Cardinal Janis Pujats
Archbishop emeritus of Riga
✠ Tomash Peta
Archbishop of the archdiocese of Saint Mary in Astana
✠ Jan Pawel Lenga
Archbishop-Bishop emeritus of Karaganda
✠ Athanasius Schneider
Auxiliary Bishop of the archdiocese of Saint Mary in Astana

*"The Church of the living God—
the pillar and bulwark of the truth."
(1 Tim 3:15)*

DECLARATION OF THE TRUTHS RELATING TO SOME OF THE MOST COMMON ERRORS IN THE LIFE OF THE CHURCH OF OUR TIME

The Fundamentals of Faith

1. The right meaning of the expressions "living tradition," "living Magisterium," "hermeneutic of continuity," and "development of the doctrine" signifies that whatever new insights there may be into the Deposit of Faith, nevertheless the content of a Catholic doctrine cannot be changed into a meaning contrary to the meaning that the Church always proposed in the same dogma, in the same sense, and in the same meaning (see First Vatican Council, *Dei Filius*, Session 3, chap. 4: "in eodem dogmate, eodem sensu, eademque sententia").

2. "The meaning of dogmatic formulas remains ever true and constant in the Church, even when it is expressed with greater clarity or more developed." Thus, the opinion is wrong that says "first, that dogmatic formulas (or some category of them) cannot signify truth in a determinate way, but can only offer

changeable approximations to it, which to a certain extent distort or alter it; secondly, that these formulas signify the truth only in an indeterminate way, this truth being like a goal that is constantly being sought by means of such approximations." I affirm, therefore, that "those who hold such an opinion do not avoid dogmatic relativism and they corrupt the concept of the Church's infallibility relative to the truth to be taught or held in a determinate way" (Sacred Congregation for the Doctrine of the Faith, Declaration *Mysterium Ecclesiae* in defense of the Catholic doctrine on the Church against certain errors of the present day, n. 5).

The Creed

3. I "confess that the Kingdom of God begun here below in the Church of Christ is not of this world whose form is passing, and that its proper growth cannot be confounded with the progress of civilization, of science, or of human technology, but that it consists in an ever more profound knowledge of the unfathomable riches of Christ, an ever stronger hope in eternal blessings, an ever more ardent response to the love of God, and an ever more generous bestowal of grace and holiness among men. The deep solicitude of the Church, the Spouse of Christ, for the needs of men, for their joys and hopes, their griefs and efforts, is therefore nothing other than her great desire to be present to them, in order to illuminate them with the light of Christ and to gather them all in Him, their only Savior. This solicitude can never mean that the Church conforms herself to the things of this world, or that she lessens the ardor of her expectation of her Lord and of the eternal Kingdom" (Paul VI, Apostolic letter *Solemni hac liturgia* [Credo of the People of

God], n. 27). The opinion is, therefore, erroneous that says that God is glorified principally by the very fact of the improvement of the temporal and earthly condition of the human race.

4. After the institution of the New and Everlasting Covenant in Jesus Christ, no one may be saved by obedience to the law of Moses without faith in Christ as the only Savior of humankind and true God (see Rom 3:28; Gal 2:16).

5. Muslims and others who lack faith in Jesus Christ, even monotheists, cannot give to God the same adoration as Christians do, that is to say, a supernatural worship in Spirit and in Truth (see Jn 4:24; Eph 2:8) of those who received the spirit of filial adoption (see Rom 8:15).

6. Spiritualities that promote any kind of idolatry or pantheism cannot be considered either as "seeds" or as "fruits" of the Divine Word already present in their worldview, since they are deceptions that preclude the evangelization and eternal salvation of their adherents, as it is taught by the Holy Scripture: "the god of this world has made blind the minds of those who have not faith, so that the light of the good news of the glory of Christ, who is the image of God, might not be shining on them" (2 Cor 4:4).

7. True ecumenism intends that non-Catholics should enter that unity which the Catholic Church already indestructibly possesses in virtue of the prayer of Christ, always heard by His Father, "that they may be one" (Jn 17:11), and which she professes in the Symbol of Faith, "I believe in one Church." Ecumenism, therefore, may not legitimately have for its goal the establishment of a united Church that does not yet exist.

8. Hell exists and that those who are condemned to hell for any unrepented mortal sin are eternally punished there by divine justice (see Mt 25:46). According to the teaching of the Holy Scripture, not only fallen angels but also human souls are damned eternally (see 2 Thes 1:9; 2 Pt 3:7). Furthermore, the eternally damned human beings will not be annihilated, since their souls are immortal according to the infallible teaching of the Church (see Fifth Lateran Council, Session 8).

9. The faith in Jesus Christ, the Incarnated Son of God and the only Savior of humankind, is the only religion positively willed by God. The opinion is, therefore, wrong that says that in the same way as God wills positively the diversity of the male and female sexes and the diversity of nations, so he wills also the diversity of religions.

10. "Our [the Christian] religion effectively establishes with God an authentic and living relationship which the other religions do not succeed in doing, even though they have, as it were, their arms stretched out towards heaven" (Paul VI, Apostolic Exhortation *Evangelii nuntiandi*, 53).

11. The gift of free will with which God the Creator endowed the human person grants man the natural right to choose only the good and the true. No human person has, therefore, a natural right to offend God in choosing the moral evil of sin or the religious error of idolatry, blasphemy, or another form of a false religion.

The Law of God

12. A justified person has the strength with God's grace to carry out the objective demands of the divine law, since all of the

commandments of God are possible for the justified. God's grace, when it justifies the sinner, does of its nature produce conversion from all serious sin, and God's grace is sufficient for conversion from all serious sin (see Council of Trent, Session 6, *Decree on Justification*, chap. 11; chap. 13).

13. "The faithful are obliged to acknowledge and respect the specific moral precepts declared and taught by the Church in the name of God, the Creator and Lord. Love of God and of one's neighbor cannot be separated from the observance of the commandments of the Covenant renewed in the blood of Jesus Christ and in the gift of the Spirit" (John Paul II, Encyclical *Veritatis Splendor*, 76). According to the teaching of the same Encyclical the opinion of those is wrong, who "believe they can justify, as morally good, deliberate choices of kinds of behavior contrary to the commandments of the divine and natural law." Thus, "these theories cannot claim to be grounded in the Catholic moral tradition" (ibid.).

14. All of the commandments of God are equally just, merciful, perfective of the rational creature, and necessary for the common good. The opinion is, therefore, wrong that says that a person is able, by obedience to a divine prohibition, to sin against God by that very act of obedience, or to harm himself, or to sin against another.

15. There are moral principles and moral truths contained in divine revelation and in the natural law which include negative prohibitions that absolutely forbid certain kinds of action, inasmuch as these kinds of action are always gravely unlawful on account of their object. Hence, the opinion is wrong that says that a good intention or a good consequence is or can ever be sufficient

to justify the commission of such kinds of action (see John Paul II, Encyclical *Veritatis Splendor*, 80).

16. A woman who has conceived a child within her womb is forbidden by natural and Divine Law to extinguish this human life within her, by herself or by others (see John Paul II, Encyclical *Evangelium Vitae*, 62).

17. Artificial procedures which cause conception to happen outside of the womb "are morally unacceptable, since they separate procreation from the fully human context of the conjugal act" (John Paul II, Encyclical *Evangelium Vitae*, 14).

18. No human being, so that he may escape temporal suffering, may ever be morally justified or morally permitted to intend to kill himself or to cause himself to be put to death by others. "Euthanasia is a grave violation of the law of God, since it is the deliberate and morally unacceptable killing of a human person. This doctrine is based upon the natural law and upon the written word of God, is transmitted by the Church's Tradition and taught by the ordinary and universal Magisterium" (John Paul II, Encyclical *Evangelium Vitae*, 65).

19. Marriage is by Divine ordinance and natural law an indissoluble union of one man and of one woman, which of its very nature is ordered to the procreation and education of offspring and to mutual love (see Gn 2:24; Mk 10:7-9; Eph 5:31-32).

20. By natural and divine law no human being may voluntarily exercise his sexual powers outside of a valid marriage without sin. It is, therefore, contrary to Holy Scripture and Tradition to affirm that conscience can truly and rightly judge that sexual acts between persons who have contracted a civil marriage with

each other, although one or both persons is sacramentally married to another person, can sometimes be morally right or requested or even commanded by God.

21. By natural and divine law, when an act of conjugal intercourse is intended or performed or has been performed, no person may legitimately seek to prevent procreation, either as an end or as a means (see Paul VI, Encyclical *Humanae Vitae*, 14).

22. Anyone, husband or wife, who has obtained a civil divorce from the spouse to whom he is validly married, and has contracted a civil marriage with some other person during the lifetime of his spouse, and who lives *more uxorio* with the civil partner, and who chooses to remain in this state with full knowledge of the nature of the act and with full consent of the will to that act, is in a state of mortal sin and can therefore not receive sanctifying grace and grow in charity. Therefore, these Christians, unless they are living as "brother and sister," cannot receive Holy Communion (see John Paul II, Apostolic Exhortation *Familiaris consortio*, 84).

23. Two persons of the same sex sin gravely when they seek venereal pleasure from each other (see Lv 18:22; 20:13; Rom 1:24–28; 1 Cor 6:9-10; 1 Tm 1:10; Jude 7). Hence, the opinion is contrary to Divine Revelation that says that as God the Creator has given to some humans a natural disposition to feel sexual desire for persons of the opposite sex, so also He has given to others a natural disposition to feel sexual desire for persons of the same sex, and that He intends that the latter disposition be acted on in some circumstances.

24. Human law, or any human power whatsoever, cannot give to two persons of the same sex the right to marry one another or declare two such persons to be so married, since this is contrary to natural and Divine law.

25. Unions that have the name of marriage without the reality of it are not capable of receiving the blessing of the Church, this being contrary to Divine law.

26. The civil power may not establish civil or legal unions between two persons of the same sex that plainly imitate the union of marriage, even if such unions do not receive the name of marriage, since such unions would encourage grave sin for the individuals who are in them and would be a cause of grave scandal for others (see Congregation for the Doctrine of the Faith, *Considerations regarding proposals to give legal recognition to unions between homosexual persons*, June 3, 2003).

27. Male and female sexes are biological realities. It is, therefore, contrary to natural and Divine law that a man may attempt to become a woman by mutilating or poisoning himself, or even by simply declaring himself to be such, or that a woman may in like manner attempt to become a man, or that the civil authority has the duty or the right to act as if such things were or may be possible and legitimate.

28. In accordance with Holy Scripture and the constant tradition of the ordinary and universal Magisterium, the Church did not err in teaching that the civil power may lawfully exercise capital punishment on malefactors where this is truly necessary to preserve the existence or just order of societies (see Gn 9:6; Jn 19:11; Rom 13:1–7).

29. All authority on earth as well as in heaven belongs to Jesus Christ; therefore, civil societies and all other associations of men are subject to his kingship so that "the duty of offering God genuine worship concerns man both individually and socially" (*Catechism of the Catholic Church*, 2105).

The Sacraments

30. In the most holy sacrament of the Eucharist, a wonderful change takes place, namely of the whole substance of bread into the body of Christ and the whole substance of wine into His blood, a change which the Catholic Church very fittingly calls transubstantiation (see Fourth Lateran Council, chap. 1; Council of Trent, Session 13, chap. 4). "Every theological explanation which seeks some understanding of this mystery must, in order to be in accord with Catholic faith, maintain that in the reality itself, independently of our mind, the bread and wine have ceased to exist after the Consecration, so that it is the adorable body and blood of the Lord Jesus that from then on are really before us under the sacramental species of bread and wine" (Paul VI, Apostolic letter *Solemni hac liturgia* [Credo of the People of God], n. 25).

31. The formulations by which the Council of Trent expressed the Church's faith in the Holy Eucharist are suitable for men of all times and places, since they are a "perennially valid teaching of the Church" (John Paul II, Encyclical *Ecclesia de Eucharistia*, 15).

32. In the Holy Mass, a true and proper sacrifice is offered to the Blessed Trinity and this sacrifice is propitiatory both for men

living on earth and for the souls in purgatory. The opinion is, therefore, wrong that says that the sacrifice of the Mass consists simply in the fact that the people make a spiritual sacrifice of prayers and praises, as well as the opinion that the Mass may or should be defined as Christ giving Himself to the faithful as their spiritual food (see Council of Trent, Session 22, chap. 2).

33. "The Mass, celebrated by the priest representing the person of Christ by virtue of the power received through the Sacrament of Orders and offered by him in the name of Christ and the members of His Mystical Body, is the sacrifice of Calvary rendered sacramentally present on our altars. We believe that as the bread and wine consecrated by the Lord at the Last Supper were changed into His body and His blood which were to be offered for us on the cross, likewise the bread and wine consecrated by the priest are changed into the body and blood of Christ enthroned gloriously in heaven, and we believe that the mysterious presence of the Lord, under what continues to appear to our senses as before, is a true, real and substantial presence" (Paul VI, Apostolic letter *Solemni hac liturgia* [Credo of the People of God], n. 24).

34. "The unbloody immolation at the words of consecration, when Christ is made present upon the altar in the state of a victim, is performed by the priest and by him alone, as the representative of Christ and not as the representative of the faithful.... and that the faithful offer the sacrifice by the hands of the priest from the fact that the minister at the altar, in offering a sacrifice in the name of all His members, represents Christ, the Head of the Mystical Body. The

conclusion, however, that the people offer the sacrifice with the priest himself is not based on the fact that, being members of the Church no less than the priest himself, they perform a visible liturgical rite; for this is the privilege only of the minister who has been divinely appointed to this office: rather it is based on the fact that the people unite their hearts in praise, impetration, expiation, and thanksgiving with prayers or intention of the priest, even of the High Priest himself, so that in the one and same offering of the victim and according to a visible sacerdotal rite, they may be presented to God the Father" (Pius XII, Encyclical *Mediator Dei*, 92–93).

35. The sacrament of Penance is the only ordinary means by which grave sins committed after Baptism may be remitted and by divine law all such sins must be confessed by number and by species (see Council of Trent, Session 14, can. 7).

36. By divine law the confessor may not violate the seal of the sacrament of Penance for any reason whatsoever; no ecclesiastical authority has the power to dispense him from the seal of the sacrament and the civil power is wholly incompetent to oblige him to do so.

37. In virtue of the will of Christ and the unchangeable tradition of the Church, the sacrament of the Holy Eucharist may not be given to those who are in a public state of objectively grave sin and sacramental absolution may not be given to those who express their unwillingness to conform to divine law, even if their unwillingness pertains only to a single grave matter.

38. According to the constant tradition of the Church, the sacrament of the Holy Eucharist may not be given to those who deny any truth of the Catholic faith by formally professing their adherence to a heretical or a schismatic Christian community.

39. The law by which priests are bound to observe perfect continence in celibacy belongs to immemorial and apostolic tradition according to the constant witness of the Fathers of the Church and of the Roman Pontiffs. For this reason this law should not be abolished in the Roman Church through the innovation of an optional priestly celibacy, either at the regional or the universal level. The perennial valid witness of the Church states that the law of priestly continence "does not command new precepts and that these precepts should be observed, because they have been neglected on the part of some through ignorance and sloth. These precepts, nevertheless, go back to the apostles and were established by the Fathers, as it is written, 'Stand firm, then, brothers and keep the traditions that we taught you, whether by word of mouth or by letter' (2 Thes 2:15). There are in fact many who, ignoring the statutes of our forefathers, have violated the chastity of the Church by their presumption and have followed the will of the people, not fearing the judgment of God" (Pope Siricius, *Decretal Cum in unum*, can. 1).

40. By the will of Christ and the Divine constitution of the Church, only baptized men (*viri*) may receive the sacrament of Orders, whether in the episcopacy, the priesthood, or the diaconate (see John Paul II Apostolic Letter, *Ordinatio Sacerdotalis*, 4). Furthermore, the assertion is wrong that says that only an Ecumenical Council can define this matter,

because the teaching authority of an Ecumenical Council is not more extensive than that of the Roman Pontiff (see Fifth Lateran Council, Session 11; First Vatican Council, Session 4, chap. 3, n. 8).

May 31, 2019
✠ Cardinal Raymond Leo Burke
Patron of the Sovereign Military Order of Malta

✠ Cardinal Janis Pujats
Archbishop emeritus of Riga

✠ Tomash Peta
Archbishop of the archdiocese of Saint Mary in Astana

✠ Jan Pawel Lenga
Archbishop-Bishop emeritus of Karaganda

✠ Athanasius Schneider
Auxiliary Bishop of the archdiocese of Saint Mary in Astana

Index

Page numbers for definitions are in boldface.

A

abortion, 121, 131, 148–**150**, 226
absolution. *See* penance
abstinence, 127–128
Acacianism. *See* Homoianism
accidents, Eucharistic. *See* Eucharist
action: heresy of (*see* Activism); in *Persona Christi*, 230; moral, 130–156
Activism, 54
acts: conjugal, 125–128, 153, 227; moral (*see* action: moral); objectively evil, 112, 121, **131**, 131n141, 139–140, 146, 225–226, 231
Adam, 73, 79, 141
adoption: grace of, 116–117 (*see also* baptism); by same-sex couples, 130
Adoptionism, **19**, 21, **22**, 77. *See also* Spanish Adoptionism
adoration, 54, 71, 78, 84–85, 111, 119, 121, 136, 144, 223. *See also* idolatry
adultery, 64, 121, 125, 126, 132n142, **153**, 154

adults, baptism of. *See* baptism
Agnosticism, **43**, 67, 76. *See also* Deism
Albigensianism. *See* Catharism
altar, 58, 230
altar server, 124, 178
Alumbrados. *See* Illuminism
Amalricism, **33**
Americanism, **48–49**
Anabaptism, **36**, 116
Anarchism, 168
anathema, 98–99
angels, 161, 169. *See also* Archangel
Anglicanism (Episcopalianism), **36–37**, 50–51. *See also* Branch Theory
animals, 13, 72, 154
Animism, **13**, 69. *See also* Ecological Mysticism; Gaianism; Totemism
Annihilationism, 72, 74, 224
anointing of the sick, 209
Anomoeanism. *See* Eunomianism

Anthropocentrism, **54–55**, 70, 184. *See also* Enlightenment Anthropocentrism

Anti-Christ, 176–178

Anti-Christianity, 109

Anti-Church, 46. *See also* Freemasonry

anti-liturgical heresy. *See* liturgical heresy

Anti-Mary, 177–178

Antinomianism, **37**, 132

apokatastasis, **22**, 23, 74, 80–81, 224

Apollinarianism, **24**, 77

apostasy, 89, **90**, 218

apostles, 18, 19, 93–95, 102, 104, 206, 208, 213, 215, 232

apostolate, Marian, 174

apostolic succession, 31, 37, 87, 88, 93–94, 102, 104, 215

Archangel: Gabriel, 165, 184; Michael, 174

Arianism, **24**, 68, 77, 101, 218. *See also* Eunomianism; Homoianism; Subordinationism

art, sacred. *See* image(s): sacred

asceticism, 26, 27, 34

assent, 100, 112, 122, 134, 142, 145, 204, 206, 213–214

astrology. *See* Determinism

Atheism, **13–14**, 67, 72, 74, 77, 143. *See also* Communism; Darwinism

atonement, 118, 153, 229–230

authority: of bishops and councils, 35–36, 95, 96–99, 104–107, 146–147, 192; of the Church, 88, 93–95, 100, 146, 191–194, 192; of the Magisterium, 63–64, 93–95, 204, 228; of Scripture, 72, 123, 205, 214, 228; of the State, 46, 47, 61, 111, 125, 148, 153, 154–155, 195–198, 228–229; of the Supreme Pontiff, 96, 102–104, 146, 201; of Tradition, 58, 59, 63–64, 72, 99, 123, 124, 214, 228

B

Baianism, **37–38**, 107–108, 108–109, 141. *See also* Quesnellism

Balthasarianism, **55**, 74, 80

baptism: in the Holy Spirit (*see* Pentecostalism); sacrament of, 23–24, 52, 89, 108, 208–209 (*see also* infant[s]: baptism of)

Basilideanism, **19–20**

Beatific Vision, 107–108

Berengarianism, **31**, 118

bestiality, **154**

Bible. *See* Scripture

Biological Determinism. *See* Determinism

bishop/episcopacy, 35–36, 44–45, 95, 96–99, 104–107, 146–147, 192, 217–219. *See also* holy orders

Bishop of Rome. *See* Supreme Pontiff

blasphemy, 55, 131, 140, 224

Blessed Trinity, 20, 27, 40, 41, 52, 67–68, 84, 84n73, 108, 229

blessing(s), 64, 90, 94, 129, 228

blindness of mind, 143, 223

blood, Christ's Eucharistic, 120n127, 229, 230

body, 74, 101; Christ's Eucharistic, 39, 41, 119–122, 229, 230; Christ's human, 24, 41, 77, 78–79; Christ's Mystical, 156, 157, 217–219,

230–231; origin of human, 72, 72n56; respect for human, 62, 73, 148–149, 152, 177, 183; unity of soul and, 72, 151, 151n168

Bogomilism, **31**

bond, marital, 125–126, 128, 200, 226–227

brain death, 151

Branch Theory, **49**

bread, Eucharistic. *See* Eucharist

Broad Church (Latitudinarian) Anglicanism, **37**

Buddhism, 68, 89, 137. *See also* Yoga; Zen

C

Calvinism, 36, **38**, 39, 108–109, 109–110, 118, 119, 141

Canon Law, 7, 101–102, 121, 124, 125, 135–136, 140n156, 147, 147n162, 150

canon of Scripture, 30, 205

capital punishment. *See* death penalty

catechesis, xiii–xiv

Catharism (Albigensianism), **32**

Catholic Church: authority of (*see under* authority); defined, 87–92; indefectibility of, 91; infallibility of (*see* infallibility); marks of (*see under* mark[s] of the Church); members of, 87–90; mission of, 88; no salvation outside (*see under* necessity); the only true, 6, 56, 87–88, 91, 191 (*see also under* mark[s] of the Church; religion); perpetuity of, 91; relations to civil society, 95, 125, 129, 148, 154–155, 191–198, 201, 229, 231; visibility of, 90, 102

catholicity. *See under* mark(s) of the Church

celibacy, 40, 201, 232

ceremonies, 19, 58, 82, 116, 119, 132, 144, 146, 156–161

certainty of justification, 27, 40, 60, 78, 135

character, sacramental. *See* sacramental character

charism(s), 91, 102, 215

charity, 5–6, 57, 98–99, 106, 126, 130, 139, 145, 178, 217, 219, 227

chastity, 143, 153–154, 183, 232. *See also* celibacy

children, 82, 116–117, 125, 127–128, 130, 148–150, 153–154, 196–197, 217, 226

choice. *See* free will

Church: Catholic (*see* Catholic Church); non-Catholic, 41, 50–51, 87, 136, 145

circumcision, 19, 132

citizen(s), 115, 148

clergy, 91, 100, 122, 147, 193, 212, 218

cohabitation, 121, 125, 153, 154

collegiality, **106**

common good, 102, 111, 132–133, 147, 153, 225

communion: with the Church, 89, 90, 98–99, 122, 136, 140n156; pope as visible sign of, 102; sacramental, 7, 64, 118, 119–122, 140n156, 150, 154, 227, 231–232

Communism, 14, **49**, 51, 154–155, 191. *See also* Neo-Adamism

conception, 150, 226; of Christ, 166, 172, 182; of Mary, 167–168, 181

Conciliarism, **35–36**, 95, 96, 96n88

concubinage. *See* cohabitation

condemnation: to death (*see* death penalty); of error, 102 (*see also* anathema; Declaration of Truths; excommunication; Syllabus of Errors; Syllabus against Modernism; *and individual heresies*); to hell, 79–81, 121, 224; of sin, 17, 19, 23, 36, 42, 62–64, 135, 149, 158–159

conscience, 42, 61, 113–115, 121, 195, 218, 226–227

consecrated life. *See* religious life

consecration, 41, 119, 179–180, 229, 230

consent, 53, 125, 127, 142, 143, 195, 227

Consequentialism, **55**, 131, 150–151, 155, 225–226

consubstantiation (impanation), **39**, 118

contemplation, 38, 205

continence, 40, 232

contraception, 126–128, 131, 150, 153

conversion, 70, 83, 107, 134, 139, 225

cooperation: in evil (*see* moral cooperation); with grace, 28, 78, 79, 80, 108–110, 134, 142

correction: of inferiors, 140, 150, 217; of superiors, 100–101

council(s): general (ecumenical, universal), 35, 46, 63, 96, 97–98, 101–102, 192, 194, 232–233; particular (local, regional), 45, 58, 97, 158–159. *See also* collegiality

Covenant: New, 82, 83, 124, 223; Old, 83, 124, 225

creation, 15, 21, 45, 54, 63, 68–74, 76, 137, 152, 170–171, 211, 213

Creator, 15, 23, 41, 63, 68–74, 79, 113, 126, 127, 156, 170–171, 208, 214, 224–225, 227

Creed, 37, 84, 87, 159, 211, 222–224

crisis, 8–9, 101, 216–220

Cross, 20, 28, 30, 33, 78, 230

culture, 71, 215

custom(s), 23–24, 105, 119, 145, 159–160, 209

D

damnation, 28, 38, 77, 79–81, 121, 141, 179, 224

Darwinism, **49**, 72

deacon/diaconate, 123–124. *See also* holy orders

deaconess, 123–124

death, 68, 72, 74, 116–117, 128, 141, 151, 177, 226. *See also* death penalty; Jesus Christ: death of; killing

death penalty, 31, 153, 228

Decalogue. *See* Ten Commandments

Declaration of Truths, 216–233

defense: civil, 153; of heresy, 203; of self, 125, 153, 155; of truth, 68, 102, 103, 120, 218

Deism, **44**, 67. *See also* Freemasonry; Positivism

Demonism. *See* Satanism

demons, 15, 17, 70, 74, 80–81, 117, 138, 144. *See also* Satan

Deposit of Faith, 93, 103, 204, 213, 221

desire(s), 38, 75, 81–82, 86, 99, 125, 131, 136, 140, 141, 145, 149, 150, 157, 173, 197, 227 despair, 134, 143, 179

Determinism, **14**, 71, 131

development, 49, 72, 75–76, 94, 107, 117–118, 147, 148, 157, 203, 210, 213, 221–222. *See also* evolution

devil. *See* demons; Satan

devotion, 165–184

Diabolism. *See* Satanism

Dialectical Materialism, **51–52**

dignity, human. *See under* man

discernment, 58, 218

discipline, 9, 69, 92, 96–97, 147n162, 158, 196, 209

divination, **14**, 144

divinity, 13, 16, 19, 24, 26, 68, 85, 101, 137, 166, 170, 207

divorce, 125–126, 128, 200, 226–227

Docetism, **18**, 77, 78

doctrine, xiii–xiv, 5–9, 67, 77, 87, 91, 93–94, 98, 102–103, 111, 182. *See also individual doctrines*

dogma, 40, 44, 58, 92, 93–94, 97, 98, 101, 109, 118, 123–124, 151n168, 167–168, 189, 192, 200, 203, 206–207, 208, 210, 212, 213–214, 221–222

Donatism, **25**. *See also* Meletianism

doubt, 7, 43, 53, 123, 135, 206

Dualism, **14**, 72, 73–74. *See also* Bogomilism; Gnosticism; Manichaeism

dulia (veneration), 30, 33, 40, 180–181

duty, 52, 61, 113, 114, 122, 152, 160, 189–190, 197, 199, 216, 218, 228, 229; and unjust commands, 101–102, 132–133. *See also* obedience

E

earth, worship of, 13, 16, 62, 69, 136–137, 144

Eastern Orthodoxy, **32**, 49, 89, 96, 122

Ecological Mysticism, **62**, 69, 144

ecumenical council. *See under* councils

Ecumenism, 56, 223

elderly, 150

Emanationism, 21, 69

end: of creation, 54–55, 70, 76, 213; of human life (*see* death); of man (*see under* man); of a moral act, 55, 126, 131, 131n141, 148–149, 150–151, 155, 225–227; of the world (*see under* time)

enemy/enemies, 98–99, 139, 150, 167–168, 176–178, 183

Enlightenment Anthropocentrism, **44**, 60

ensoulment. *See* conception

Episcopalianism. *See* Anglicanism

Episcopalism, **44–45**, 96. *See also* Febronianism; Gallicanism; Josephinism

error(s): of conscience (*see* conscience); invincible (innocent, inculpable), 85–86, 114, 131, 135; vincible (culpable), 126, 135, 136, 150–151, 225–226

eschaton. *See* last things

eternity, 22, 80–81, 108

Eucharist, 31, 41, 57, 58, 118–119, 146–147, 209, 229–231. *See also* Communion: sacramental

eugenics, 71

Eunomianism (Anomoeanism, Heteroousianism), **25**

euthanasia, 131, 150, 226
Eutychianism. *See* Monophysitism
Evangelical (Low Church) Anglicanism, **37**
Evangelical Lutheranism. *See* Lutheranism
Eve, 165
evil, 5, 6, 129, 176–178; freedom from all (*see* heaven); leading another to (*see* scandal); spirits (*see* demons)
evolution, 19–20, 49, 64, 72–73, 91, 209, 210, 211, 213
ex cathedra, 96, 97, 102, 103–104
excommunication, 89, **90**, 140n156; those who incur (or incurred), 19, 21, 23, 27, 28, 33, 39, 136n148, 203; when unjust, 90, 90n83. *See also* anathema
execution. *See* death penalty
Existentialism, **55–56**
experience, not determining truth, 50, 60, 62, 117. *See also* conscience; Modernism
expiation, 208, 231

F

Faith: Deposit of (*see* Deposit of Faith); supernatural (theological), 8, 57, 90, 108, 172–174. *See also* Creed
Fall, 75. *See also* Original Sin
False Ecumenism (Irenism), **56**, 223
false worship. *See under* worship
family, 56, 71, 88, 128, 132. *See also* marriage
fasting, 27
Fatalism. *See* Determinism

Father, first Person of the Trinity, 20, 22, 24, 25–26, 27, 33, 68, 76, 85, 86, 110, 137, 156, 160, 176, 223, 231. *See also* Blessed Trinity
Fathers of the Church, 6–7, 20, 86, 120n127, 203, 213, 215, 232
fear, 80, 169, 173, 183, 232
feast(s), 187
Febronianism, **45**, 47. *See also* Josephinism
Feminism, **56**, 71, 177
Fideism (Traditionalism), **50**
fidelity, 57, 83, 100–101, 103, 132, 158, 166, 171, 173, 213, 215
fire, 7, 8
flesh, Eucharistic (*see under* body)
forgiveness of sins, 23, 134–135, 135n147, 231
form, sacramental. *See* sacramental form
formula(s), 15, 39, 58, 118, 159, 212–215, 221–222, 229
fornication, 131, 153. *See also* cohabitation
fraternity, 45–46, 88, 106, 217, 219
Fraticelli, **34**
freedom, 39–40, 71, 112, 179, 224
freedom, religious. *See* religious liberty
freedom, unlimited, 61, 73–74, 112–115, 113n116, 179, 190–191
Freemasonry, 44, **45–46**, 135–136, 136n148, 174–176. *See also* Josephinism
free will, 13, 109–110, 134, 142, 224. *See also* Determinism; freedom; Original Sin
friend(s), 125

Index

fulfillment, 82, 83, 104

future, 14, 22, 57, 91, 97, 213

G

Gaianism, 62, 136–137

Gallicanism, 45, **46–47**, 95, 96. *See also* Josephinism

gender ideology, **62–63**, 73–74, 152, 177. *See also* Transgenderism

gender theory. *See* gender ideology

Genesis, 69, 211

Gentiles, 205

gesture(s), 137. *See also* ceremonies

Gnosticism, **15**, 18, 19, 20, 72, 72n56, 74, 77, 138–139. *See also* Antinomianism; Basilideanism; Bogomilism; Freemasonry; Manichaeism; Montanism; Mormonism; New Age; Priscillianism; Tondrakianism; Valentinianism

God. *See* adoration; Blessed Trinity; divinity; *and individual Persons of the Blessed Trinity*

good: common (*see* common good); moral, 59, 131, 149, 224; works (*see under* works)

goodness, 34, 70, 83, 112, 142, 180

good news. *See* Gospel(s)

goods. *See* property

Gospel(s), 30, 98, 100, 104, 167, 179, 205–206; and the New Law, 207, 210

grace: actual, 132, 134, 139, 169, 175, 219, 222, 224–225; habitual (*see* sanctifying grace); state of (*see* sanctifying grace)

Gradualism, **57**, 132

gratitude, 127, 173

guilt, 126, 135, 136, 150–151, 225–226

H

habit(s), 108, 130, 156, 180. *See also* custom(s); virtue(s); *and individual virtues*

hatred, 140, 143, 175

head, 37, 76, 104, 123, 156, 161, 165, 176, 178, 181–182, 210, 217, 230

healing, 138

health, 98–99, 144, 147–149, 216, 219. *See also* medical products

heart, 55, 71, 173, 175, 182, 214, 219, 231

heaven, 41, 74, 79–80, 107–108, 129, 131, 169–170, 173, 206, 230

Hedonism, **15**, 144, 198

hell, 22, 55, 74, 80–81, 91, 169, 172–173, 179, 224

heresy: definition of, **6–7**; Destroyer of, Mary, 165–184; gravity of, 5–6; mystery of, 7–9; synthesis of all (*see* Modernism). *See also individual heresies*

Heteroousianism. *See* Eunomianism

hierarchy, 27, 36–37, 40, 101, 106, 122–124, 157, 158, 161, 210, 213, 216

High Church Anglicanism, 37

Hinduism, 68, 89, 137

history, 6–9, 44, 51, 57, 59, 69, 69n50, 91, 143, 159, 160, 165–166, 180, 183, 204, 205, 207, 209, 214, 215

holiness, 9, 54, 57, 76, 111, 117, 157–158, 222; mark of the Church (*see under* mark[s] of the Church)

holy day(s), 19, 27, 146

holy orders, 36–37, 119, 122–124, 177–178, 230, 232–233

Holy Spirit, 20, 26, 27, 34, 41, 68, 85–86, 92, 94, 103, 105, 118, 182, 209. *See also* Blessed Trinity

Homoianism (Acacianism), **25–26**

Homoiousianism (Semi-Arianism), 25, **26**

homosexual: activism, 63, 121, 143, 154; acts (*see* sodomy); attraction/inclination, 63, 74, 143, 227; ideology, **63**, 64, 121, 129–130, 143, 153–154, 227–228

honor, 35, 85, 121, 136, 144, 155, 181, 219

hope, 7, 55, 57, 79, 80, 139, 166, 172, 180, 183, 191, 222

host, sacred (Eucharistic), 120

humanity, 18, 45–46, 88, 110, 165–167

humility, 157, 169, 181

husband. *See* marriage

Hussitism, **34–35**

hypostatic union. *See* Jesus Christ: fully God and fully man

I

icon(s), 30

Iconoclasm (Iconomachy), **30**

Iconomachy. *See* Iconoclasm

idolatry, 30, 62, 69, 71, 110, 131, **136**–139, **144**–145, 223, 224. *See also* Paganism; Pantheism

idols. *See* idolatry

ignorance, 84, 85–86, 131, 205, 232

illness, 68, 150, 151, 152

Illuminati. *See* Illuminism

Illuminism (Alumbrados), **38–39**

image(s): man in God's, 64; sacred, 30, 40, 178

Immaculate Conception, 167–168, 187

immortality, 31, 64, 70, 72, 224

immunity, 113, 113n116, 193, 195

immutability, 76, 94, 132, 210, 211, 215, 218

impanation (consubstantiation), **39**, 118

impeccability, 103

impediments, 200

impetration. *See* supplication

imposition of hands, 23

Incarnation, 33, 53, 108, 120, 166; errors about, 40, 75–77 (*see also* Adoptionism; Apollinarianism; Arianism; Docetism; Gnosticism; Monophysitism; Monotheletism; Nestorianism)

incredulity. *See* unbelief

indissolubility of marriage. *See under* marriage

Individualism, 111

indulgence(s), 33, 40

inerrancy of Scripture, 189, 205, 211, 214

infallibility, 127n120; of the Church, 81, 91, 93, 95, 96–97, 123, 130, 158, 222, 224; of ecumenical councils, 63, 97–98; of the pope, 95–97, 102–104

infant(s): baptism of, 33, 36, 40, 116–117, 209; prenatal murder of (*see* abortion)

infidelity, 101, 173

initiation, 15

Index

injustice, 16, 141, 153, 188, 199
inspiration, 6, 21, 37, 41, 205
institution: of the Church, 8, 86, 87, 88, 107, 213; of the sacraments (*see individual sacraments*)
intellect, 32, 43, 107–108, 141, 144, 183
intention, 29, 55, 57, 126, 127, 131, 131n141, 148–149, 150–151, 155, 208, 225–227, 231
intercession, 165, 181, 184, 218–220
interior life. *See* spiritual life
interpretation, 8, 36, 37, 57, 93, 151n168, 203–212, 214
intoxication, 144
intrinsically evil acts. *See* acts: objectively evil
invocation, 165, 181, 184, 218–220
Irenism. *See* False Ecumenism
irreligion, 143. *See also* Atheism
Islam, 16, 68, 84–85, 84n71, 88, 223
IVF (in vitro fertilization), 128, 149, 150, 226

J

Jansenism, 38, **42**, 58, 108–109, 109–110, 141, 142, 158–159. *See also* Quesnellism
Jesus Christ: always sinless and holy, 141; Bridegroom, 122, 123, 182; death of, 20, 42, 57, 78, 79, 208; divinity of, 18, 19, 20, 22, 27, 30–31, 41, 77, 79, 85, 119, 144, 166, 176, 207; doctrine of, xiii, 87, 122, 166, 205, 207, 211, 215; faith in, 19, 36, 78, 82–83, 84, 166, 208, 223, 224; fully God and fully man, 77, 104, 122, 166, 224; Head of the Church (*see* head); humanity of, 18, 19, 24, 27, 30–31, 77, 78, 110, 207–208, 229; Judge, 217, 218; King, 78, 106, 111, 160–161, 229; Lawgiver, 78, 231, 232; life of, 206, 207, 208; Messiah, 57, 82, 176, 207, 208; Passion of, 20, 118, 230; personhood of, 19, 20, 22, 28, 29, 30–31, 41, 77, 189, 207, 230; Real Presence (Eucharistic) of, 31, 41, 118–119, 229–230; Redeemer, 42, 76, 78, 80, 82; Resurrection of, 79, 208; Savior, 83, 222, 223, 224; Teacher, 41, 77, 94, 207, 211, 215. *See also* Blessed Trinity
Joachimism, **34**
Josephinism, 45, **47**
Jovinianism, **26**
Judaism, Rabbinic/Talmudic, 16, 68, **82**–83, 88, 132, 137
Judaizing, **19**, 132
judgment, 41, 46, 48, 67, 95, 100, 113, 123, 135–136, 190, 192, 195, 203, 204, 215, 226–227; particular, 121, 137, 217, 218, 232; general (universal), 166, 217, 232
jurisdiction, 44–45, 46, 96–97, 105, 132, 133, 194, 198
justice, 224; as holiness (*see* justification; sanctifying grace); social, 71, 115, 152
justification, 37–38, 40, 60–61, **78**, 130, 142, 224–225

K

Kardecism, **17**
killing: the aggressor (*see* defense); the criminal (*see* death penalty); the innocent (*see* murder); the preborn (*see* abortion); the self (*see*

suicide); the suffering directly (*see* euthanasia)

Kingdom of God, 210, 222–223

Kingship of Christ (*see* Jesus Christ: King)

knowledge, 71, 101, 174, 196–197, 203, 207; esoteric, 15, 21, 22, 138 (*see also* Gnosticism); of the future, 14; of God, 44, 50, 76, 138, 170, 208–209, 217, 222; heresy as obstacle to, 5–9; and moral act, 131, 227; of the truth, 86, 188

L

labor, 106, 110, 168, 173, 217

laity, 59, 100, 101, 160–161, 197, 217–218

language(s), 58, 158–159, 179. *See also* semantics; words

Last Supper, 118, 230

last things, 74. *See also* death; heaven; hell; judgment; purgatory

Latitudinarian (Broad Church) Anglicanism, **37**

Latitudinarianism, **50–51**, 190–191

latria, 78, 84–85, 111, 119, 121, 136, 144, 223

law: eternal (divine), 57, 71, 78, 90, 104, 105–106, 114, 129–130, 132–134, 143, 146, 152, 199, 224–229, 231; human, 132–133, 198, 228; natural, 49, 57, 112–113, 129–130, 132–133, 143, 152, 198, 225–228 (*see also* order: of nature); New (Christian), 81, 210; Old (Mosaic), 19, 76, 81–82, 123, 132; unjust (*see* duty: and unjust commands)

laying on of hands. *See* imposition of hands

Laxism, 40, **42**

lector, 124, 178

lex credendi, 133

lex orandi, 133

lex vivendi, 133

LGBTQ+ ideology, 154, 177

Liberalism, 111, 187, 132, 202, 212

liberation theology, **57**

liberty. *See* freedom

liberty, religious, **61**, 112–115, 113n116, 190–191

lie(s), 155. *See also* lying

life: after death (*see* last things); of Christ (*see under* Jesus Christ); conjugal (*see* marriage); consecrated/religious (*see* religious life); defense of (*see* defense); eternal (*see* heaven); of grace, 132, 134, 139, 169, 175, 219, 222, 224–225 (*see also* sanctifying grace); interior or spiritual (*see* spiritual life); moral (*see* action: moral; moral cooperation); respect for human, 149 (*see also* abortion; euthanasia; IVF; suicide)

light, 7, 14, 107, 114–115, 172, 173, 190, 213, 222, 223

liturgical heresy (anti-liturgical heresy), **58**, 144–145, 157, 158–159

liturgy, 99n93, 124, **156**, 178, 209, 229–233; errors about, 40, 58, 63–64, 118–124, 133, 145–148, 156–161; sacredness of, 90, 118–124, 145, 156–161

Lollardism, **35**

Lord. *See* adoration; Blessed Trinity; divinity; *and individual Persons of the Blessed Trinity*

Index

love: of enemies, 98–99; supernatural (theological) (*see* charity)

Low Church (Evangelical) Anglicanism, 37

lust, 67, 140, 142–143, 153–154, 179

Lutheranism, **39**, 108–109, 118, 139, 141–142

lying, 27, 131, 155–156

M

Macedonianism, **26**, 68

magic, **15**, 144

Magisterial Positivism, **63–64**, 95, 100

Magisterium, 46, 61, 63–64, 64n47, 69, 81, 91, 93–95, 97, 99, 100, 109, 112, 115, 123, 149, 187, 204, 216, 221, 226, 228

major orders. *See* bishop/episcopacy; holy orders; priesthood

man: creation of, 15, 19–20, 23, 49, 63, 68–70, 72–74, 79, 224, 227; dignity of, 54–55, 60–61, 64, 69–70, 70n51, 71–74, 102, 107–108, 110, 112, 122–123, 128, 141–142, 148–155, 177, 224, 226; end of, 5, 53–56, 64, 70, 70n51, 74, 107–108, 110, 111, 123, 128, 149, 177, 191, 217, 224 (*see also* end: of creation)

Manichaeism, **22–23**. *See also* Priscillianism

Marcionism, **20**

marijuana, 144

mark(s) of the Church, 49, 87–88; apostolic, 31, 37, 49, 88, 213; catholic, 6, 86, 88, 157; holy, 87–88, 92, 157; one, 6, 56, 87, 223

marriage, 31, 32, 56, 63, 71, 125–130, 131, 142, 177, 199–201, 226–228

Mary, Blessed Virgin, 26, 28, 30, 141, 165–184, 220

Marxism, 14, **51**, 57, 155. *See also* Communism; Socialism

Masonic associations. *See* Freemasonry

Mass, 40, 63–64, 118–122, 146–148, 156–161, 229–231

masturbation, 142, 153, 226–227

Materialism, 49, **51–52**, 71, 72, 74, 150, 167

matrimony. *See* marriage

media, 140, 156, 176, 179

mediation, 80, 85–86, 169

Mediator, 76

Mediatrix, 169

medical products, 144, 148–149, 151

medicine, 151–152. *See also* medical products

meditation, 137–138, 176–177, 205

Meletianism, **27**

members of the Church (*see* Catholic Church: members of)

mercy, 134, 139, 170, 225,

merit(s), 7, 42, 80, 82, 108, 131, 139, 170

Messiah. *See* Jesus Christ: Messiah

metempsychosis. *See* Reincarnationism

Methodism (Wesleyanism), **47**

minister(s), of the sacraments, 116, 122–124, 178, 230–232. *See also individual sacraments*

ministry, 8, 25, 102, 106, 107, 123, 124, 207, 217, 219

miracles, 92, 189, 206, 207, 213

mission, 51, 76, 88, 104–105, 107, 122, 160, 169, 179, 195–196, 210

missionary, 137

Modalism (Sabellianism, Patripassianism), **20**, 21

Modernism, 54–55, **58**, 59, 67, 68, 89, 91, 99, 115, 116; Oath against, 212–215; Syllabus against, 202–212

modesty, 140

Mohammedanism. *See* Islam

Molinism (Quietism), 39, **42–43**

Monarchianism, **21**. *See also* Adoptionism; Modalism

monarchy, 22, 27, 45, 106

money, 85, 179

Monism, **16**

monk(s), 26, 28, 29, 34, 39. *See also* religious life

Monophysism. *See* Monophysitism

Monophysitism (Monophysism), **27**, 77. *See also* Monotheletism

Monotheletism, **29**, 77

Montanism, **21**, 117

moral cooperation, 129–130, 145–146, 148–152, 199, 217, 228

morality, 42–43, 59, 130–156. *See also* action: moral; end: of a moral act; moral cooperation

moral law. *See* law

Moral Relativism, 42, **59**, 74, 131

Mormonism, **52**, 91

mortal sin, 7, 126, 132, 134–135, 224, 227

mortification. *See* asceticism

Moses, 75–76, 83, 223

murder, 55, 131, 148–151, 153

Muslim(s). *See* Islam

mutilation, 152, 228

mysteries, 5–9, 38, 53, 75, 79, 108, 121, 161, 170, 172, 189, 203, 205, 229, 230

mystic(al), 18, 38, 42–43, 58, 59, 62, 69, 79, 205. *See also* mysteries; spiritual life

mythology, 51, 72, 72n56, 136, 189

N

name(s), 13, 32, 38, 39, 47, 76, 80, 129, 183, 207, 228, 230

nation. *See* state(s)

Natural Family Planning, 126–128

Naturalism, 44, 45, **47**, 67, 108, **109**, 184, 188–189. *See also* Materialism; Positivism

natural law. *See under* law

nature(s): in Christ (*see* Jesus Christ: fully God and fully man); divine (*see* divinity); human (*see* man)

necessity: of baptism, 108, 116–117, 208; of the Church, 86–87; of faith, 77, 83, 108, 223; of good works, 47, 108–109, 139; of grace, 28, 54, 108, 134, 139; of observing divine law (*see under* obedience); of the sacraments (*see individual sacraments*)

necromancy, **17**

neighbor, 55, 155, 225

Neo-Adamism, **34**

Neo-Paganism, **59**, 139. *See also* New Age; Reiki; Yoga

Neo-Pelagianism, **110**

Nestorianism, **28**, 31, 77
New Age, 17, 59, 136–137, 138–139, 144
New Testament, 20, 98, 178, 189, 204. *See also* Gospel(s)
new world order, 139. *See also* Globalism.
Nicene Creed. *See* Creed
Nominalism, **32**
nourishment. *See* food
Nouvelle theologie, **59–60**
Novatianism, **23**

O

oath(s), 31, 147n164, 158, 158n180, 199; against Modernism, 212–215
obedience, 63–64, 71, 78, 85, 90, 90n83, 95, 100–101, 103, 104, 111, 132–134, 167–168, 169, 197, 199, 223, 225
object, 5, 13, 18, 112, 136, 142, 149, 170, 171, 173, 189, 206, 207, 225–226
objective, 53–54
objectively evil act(s). *See under* acts
obligation. *See* duty
obstinacy, 7, 80, 89, 135, 140, 140n156, 150, 211
occasion of sin, 139, 146
Occultism, **15**, 144
old age. *See* elderly
Old Testament, 15, 20, 30, 82, 98, 189, 204, 205
omission, sins of, 139–140, 148, 150–151
omnipotence, 68, 156
Onanism. *See* masturbation

one: true Church (*see under* Catholic Church; religion); true Faith (*see under* Catholic Church; religion); true God, 69, 71, 84, 95n87, 108, 144–145, 223; true religion (*see under* religion); true worship, 81–82, 144–146, 157–159

order, 158–159, 168, 171–172, 228; of nature, 45–46, 47, 62, 63, 122–123, 128, 152, 153–154, 168 (*see also* law: natural); new world (*see* new world order); religious (*see* religious life)

orders, holy. *See* holy orders
Origenism, **23**
Original Sin, 28, 38, 40, 52, 68, 70, 73, 75, 116, 141–142, 165, 167–168, 179
Orthodox, **32**, 49, 89, 96, 122
ownership. *See* property

P

Paganism, 54, 62, 69, 88, **89**, 110, 136, 144. *See also* Neo-Paganism; New Age; Reiki; Yoga
pain. *See* suffering
Pantheism, **16**, 43, 45, 52, 68, 69, 188–189, 215, 233. *See also* Amalricism; Animism; Valentinianism
parents, 71, 86, 99, 122, 125, 126, 128, 157, 183; first, 68, 73 (*see also* Adam; Eve)
Parousia. *See* Second Coming of Christ
passion(s), 67, 110, 143, 179; of Christ (*see under* Jesus Christ)
patriarchs, 23, 75, 101, 171, 172
Patripassianism. *See* Modalism
Paulicianism, **30**
peace, 74, 88, 180–181, 183

247

pederasty, **153**
pedophilia, 153–154
Pelagianism, **28**, 108, 116, 139, 141. *See also* Neo-Pelagianism; Semi-Pelagianism
penance, 23, 139, 209, 231. *See also* asceticism
Pentecost, 13
Pentecostalism, **60**, **117**
perfection, 33, 38–39, 42–43, 64, 69–70, 110, 171, 189, 213
perjury, 131
persecution, 23, 30, 49, 181–182
person(s): of the Blessed Trinity (*see* Blessed Trinity; *and individual Persons of the Blessed Trinity*); of Christ (*see under* Jesus Christ); human (*see* man)
perversion, 8, 45–46, 140, 154, 176
Peter, St., 87, 94–95, 102, 104, 107, 133–134, 210, 213; Successor(s) of, 87, 102–105, 213 (*see also* Supreme Pontiff)
petition. *See* supplication
Petrobrusianism, **33**
philosophy, 13–14, 17, 20, 32, 44, 50, 52, 53–54, 55–56, 59–60, 67, 68, 69, 70, 188–190, 196, 198, 202–203, 213
piety, 34, 99, 120, 183
pleasure, 15, 142, 143, 144, 178, 180, 198, 227
Pneumatomachians. *See* Macedonianism
polygamy, 52
Polygenism, 73
Polytheism, 16, **17**

pope. *See* Supreme Pontiff
pornography, 140, 153, 154, 179
Positivism, **52**. *See also* Magisterial Positivism
poverty, 33, 34, 57, 88
power(s), 15, 32, 68, 79, 80, 108, 112, 141–142, 144, 165–184, 226–227; civil (*see under* authority); ecclesiastical (*see under* authority)
praise, 118, 168, 199, 230, 231
prayer, 5, 54, 67, 99, 99n93, 107, 110, 117, 118, 147, 159, 165, 180, 184, 223, 230, 231; for the dead, 33, 40; erroneous, 84, 84n71, **110**, 137–138, 144–146 (*see also* worship: false)
preaching, 33, 93–94, 98, 104, 107, 115, 146, 168, 179, 205, 212, 215
precepts of the Church, 78, 146, 225, 232
Predestinarianism, **28**. *See also* Calvinism
presbyterate. *See* priest; priesthood
presence, Eucharistic. *See under* Jesus Christ
presumption, 139, 232
pride, 67, 169, 176
priest, 25, 106, 118–119, 160, 178, 210, 217, 218. *See also* priesthood
priesthood, 36–37, 82, 119, 122–124, 177–178, 230–233. *See also* priest
primacy, papal, 32, 35–36, 40, 44–45, 48, 102, 210
Priscillianism, **27**
private property. *See* property
Probabilism, **39–40**. *See also* Laxism
procreation, 71, 126–128, 142, 152, 226–227

Index

progress, 45–46, 111, 159, 188, 190, 193, 202, 203, 211, 213, 222

promise(s), 82, 83, 91, 94, 103, 158, 166, 169–170, 172, 215

propaganda, 35, 156

property, 33, 34, 35, 49, 51, 53–54, 154–155, 192, 197–198

prophecy, 8, 21, 79, 82, 189, 213, 219

prophet(s), 171. *See also* prophecy

propitiation. *See* atonement

Proportionalism, **55**, 131n141. *See also* Gradualism

prostitution, **153**

Protestantism, 33, 34–35, 37–38, **40**–**41**, 45, 48, 58, 74, 78, 89, 90–91, 95, 100, 115–116, 118–119, 122, 168, 191, 212. *See also* Anabaptism; Calvinism; Lutheranism; Methodism; Pentecostalism; Zwinglianism

providence, 7–9, 75, 92, 101, 171, 178, 203, 210

prudence, 95, 125, 155

public sinners, 121, 140, 150, 154

punishment, 31, 81, 100, 121, 141, 147, 150, 169, 173, 224, 228

purgatory, 33, 40, 74, 229–230

purity, 176, 182–184, 203. *See also* chastity

Q

Quesnellism, **48**

Quietism (Molinism), 39, **42–43**

R

Rabbinic Judaism. *See* Judaism, Rabbinic/Talmudic

Rahnerism, **60–61**

rape, **153**

Rationalism, 37, 44, **48**, 167, 188–190, 214. *See also* Protestantism; Semirationalism

reason, 8, 22, 43, 44, 109, 125, 127, 133–134, 144, 145, 188–190; and faith, 50, 70, 74, 75, 108, 110, 114, 143, 154, 168, 188–190, 213; and the passions, 67, 110, 143; use of, 108. *See also* Rationalism

rebaptism, **23–24**

reconciliation. *See* penance

Redemption, 40, 60–61, 75, 78–81, 172, 211. *See also* Jesus Christ: Redeemer

Reiki, 59, 136, **138**

Reincarnationism (metempsychosis, Transmigrationism), **17**, 74

Relativism, 56, 60, 74, 76, 131, 184, 222. *See also* Moral Relativism; subjectivism

religion(s): Catholic (*see* Catholicism; religion: one true); defined, 75–76; false, 52, 81–87, 95n87, 112–113, 113n116, 114–115, 117–118, 224 (*see also* worship: false); one true, 52, 76, 81–82, 85–86, 111, 166, 168, 192, 202, 224 (*see also* Catholic Church: the only true); world, 22–23, 45–46, 61, 83–84, 139

religious freedom. *See* religious liberty

Religious Indifferentism, **52**, 61, 76–77, 80, 81, 83–84, 114–115, 190–191, 202, 224

religious liberty (freedom), **61**, 95n87, 112–115, 113n116, 190–191, 202, 224

religious life, 47, 48, 53, 125, 197–198. *See also* virginity

Religious Pluralism, **61**, 76, 81, 191, 224

remission of sin, 23, 134–135, 135n147, 231

renunciation, 32. *See also* religious life

reparation, 150, 153, 218

reprobation, 191, 214

reservation, mental, 155

responsibility. *See* duty

rest, 19

Resurrection: of Christ (*see under* Jesus Christ); of the dead, 79

revelation, 188, 189, 190, 206, 211, 225–226; defined, 75–76; response to (*see* Faith); sources of, 75–76, 93, 103, (*see also* Scripture; Tradition). *See also* Deposit of Faith

reward: eternal (*see* heaven; hell); of grace for good works (*see* merit)

right(s), **112**: of Christ/God, 113, 120, 147, 148; of citizens, 49, 71, 112–115, 113n116, 151, 153, 154–155, 189–190, 199, 202, 224, 228; of conscience (*see* conscience); of the Church, 104, 148, 191–194, 195–198, 200–202, 204; of the faithful, 101–102, 107, 112, 120, 147, 160, 171; of the preborn, 149; of the State, 153, 195–198, 228

rite(s), 58, 63–64, 119, 145, 147, 147n164, 157–161, 157n178, 208, 209, 231

Roman Pontiff. *See* Supreme Pontiff

Roman Rite, 63–64, 158–161, 165

Rome, 87, 174–175, 194

Rosary, 180–181

S

Sabbath, 19, 146

Sabellianism. *See* Modalism

Sacrament(s), 94, 140, 140n156, 157n178, 158–160, 178, 229–233; errors about, 25, 30, 38, 91, 115–130, 147, 195–196, 199–201, 208–210 (*see also* Protestantism). *See also individual sacraments*

sacramental character, 89, 116, 209

sacramental form, 200

sacramentals, 30, 33, 40, 120

sacred art. *See* image(s): sacred

sacrifice(s), 178; of Christ on the Cross, 20, 172, 230; of the Mass, 40, 58, 118–119, 229–231; in the Old Testament, 82, 172

sacrilege, 120, 140,

saint(s), veneration of. *See* veneration

salvation: baptism and (*see under* necessity); Church and (*see under* necessity); faith and (*see under* necessity); good works and (*see under* necessity); grace and (*see under* necessity)

same-sex attraction, 63, 74, 143, 227

sanctification, 87–88, 92, 94, 146, 157, 160. *See also* sanctifying grace; spiritual life

sanctifying grace, 7, 60–61, 82, 108–110, 126, 131, 132, 142, 227. *See also* justification; *and individual sacraments*

sanctuary, 160

Satan, 17, 22, 61, 70–71, 74, 110, 165, 169, 174, 176, 182

Satanism (Diabolism, Demonism), **17**, 61, 71, 73–74. *See also* magic

satisfaction. *See* atonement

Savior. *See* Jesus Christ: Savior

Index

scandal, 91, 92, 129, 130, 133–134, **139–140**, 145, 146, 150, 179, 228

schism, 25, 27, 32, 35–36, 87, **89**–90, 122, 232

school(s), 20, 37, 74, 196–197, 212, 226. *See also* teacher(s)

science, 67–74. *See also* Deism, Naturalism, Rationalism

Scientism, 67–74, 198. *See also* Deism, Naturalism, Rationalism

Scripture, 72, 93, 98, 123, 223, 224, 226–227, 228; errors about, 40, 41, 51, 63, 189, 203–208, 209, 211, 214; inerrant (*see* inerrancy of Scripture); inspired (*see* inspiration). *See also* Gospel(s)

seal of the confessional, 231. *See also* sacramental character

Second Coming of Christ, 88

secret, 14, 15, 45–46, 144, 155, 191, 231

sects, 18, 19, 27, 30, 31, 32, 34, 39, 40, 45–46, 68, 78, 136n148, 145, 191

seder meals, 132

Sedevacantism, **62**, 89

See, Holy, 49, 136n148, 137, 193, 197

self-defense. *See* defense

selfishness, 127–128

self-mastery. *See* asceticism

semantics, 26, 49, 64, 93–94, 159, 213, 221

Semi-Arianism. *See* Homoiousianism

seminaries, 196, 212

Semi-Pelagianism, **29**

Semiquietism, 43

Semirationalism: Guentherian system, **53**; Hermesian system, **53**

sense(s): bodily, 173–174, 230; of the Faith (*sensus fidei*), 100; of the faithful (*sensus fidelium*), 157, 182, 218

separation, 6, 31, 40, 58, 87, 89, 98–99, 128, 225, 226; of Church and State, 111, 198; of spouses, 125–126

service(s), 124, 136, 145, 178, 179, 193

sexual complementarity, 63, 71, 152, 177

sexual disorientation, 62–63, 64, 73–74, 121, 129–130, 143, 152–154, 177, 227–228

sexual orientation, 74

Shamanism, 15

shepherd(s), 8, 91, 94, 96–97, 105–106, 140, 146, 150, 217–219

sickness. *See* illness

sign(s), 58, 102, 116, 155, 177, 207, 221–222. *See also* symbol

silence, 161, 217

simplicity, 68, 158–159, 182, 205

sin(s): consequences of, 7, 67, 68, 70, 80–81, 98–99, 141–143, 179, 183 (*see also* punishment; purgatory); forgiveness of (*see* forgiveness of sin); inclination to (*see* concupiscence); leading others to (*see* scandal); mortal (*see* mortal sin); Original (*see* Original Sin); venial (*see* venial sin)

slander. *See* calumny

slavery, 174, 179–180

sloth, 216, 219, 232

sobornost (synodalism), 96

Socialism, 51, **53–54**, 154–155, 191

society, 195–198; Christ the King of, 78, 111, 160, 229; Church as a perfect and divine, 191–194, 210,

222–223; defense of (*see* defense: civil). *See also* Catholic Church; marriage

sodomy, 63–64, 143, **153**

Son of God. *See* Jesus Christ

sorcery, 15, 144

soul(s): care/sanctification of, 5–7, 82, 87–88, 100, 107–110, 125, 140, 141, 147, 147n162, 152, 160, 173–174, 179, 182–183, 216, 224, 229–230 (*see also* sanctifying grace); of Christ, 24, 77; human, 17, 22, 23, 38, 43, 71, 74, 107–108, 177, 224; immortality of, 31, 72, 74, 224; indelibly marked (*see* sacramental character); poor in purgatory (*see* purgatory); unity of body and, 72, 151, 151n168

Spanish Adoptionism, **30–31**

species, Eucharistic, 118, 229–230

spirit(s): angels (*see* angels); fallen and evil (*see* demons); of man (*see* soul[s]: human)

spiritual exercises, 99, 137–138, 144, 202. *See also* prayer; Rosary

spiritual life, 54, 111. *See also* grace; prayer; sanctification; sanctifying grace

spontaneous generation, 68

spouse(s), 125–128, 222, 227. *See also* Jesus Christ: Bridegroom

state(s): of original justice and holiness, 34, 37–38; of grace (*see* sanctifying grace); powers of (*see under* authority); relationship to Church (*see under* authority; Catholic Church); of sin, 68, 131, 132, 134, 136, 141–143 (*see also* mortal sin)

Statism, 95

sterilization, 126, 150

subjectivism, 55–56, 117. *See also* Relativism

Subordinationism, **27**. *See also* Arianism

subsidiarity, 155

suffering, 68, 144, 150–151, 167, 169, 216, 219, 226; of Christ (*see under* Jesus Christ); eternal (*see* hell)

suicide, 32, 226

Sunday, 19, 27, 146

supernatural, 16, 37–38, 47, 53, 54, 60, 75–76, 81, 108–109, 190, 205, 208, 214–215, 218, 223

superstition, 138, 144–145. *See also* idolatry; Judaizing; magic; Syncreticism; worship: false

supplication, 180–181, 183–184, 231

Supreme Pontiff: authority of (*see under* authority); infallibility of (*see under* infallibility). *See also under* Peter, St.

surrogacy, 128

Syllabus of Errors, 187–202

Syllabus against Modernism, 202–212

symbol, 30, 40–41, 79, 124, 136, 160, 223. *See also* Creed; sign(s)

Syncreticism, 59, 110, 136

synod. *See under* council(s)

synodalism. See *sobornost*

synodality, 96, **106**–107. *See also* Episcopalism; Gallicanism

systems, moral, 15, 39–40, 42, 44, 55, 57, 131

T

Talmudic Judaism. *See* Judaism, Rabbinic/Talmudic

teacher(s), 8, 17, 19, 38, 67, 77, 94, 102, 106, 109, 171, 179, 190, 192, 196, 212, 213, 214–215, 217; Christ as (*see* Jesus Christ: Teacher). *See also* Magisterium; Modernism: Oath against; school(s)

technocracy, **155**

technology, 64, 69–70, 155, 176, 222

temple, 46, 54, 82, 110

temptation, 112, 139, 179

Ten Commandments, 15, 71, 78, 104, 130, 132, 134, 224–225

Testament: New (*see* New Testament); Old (*see* Old Testament)

thanksgiving, 231. *See also* gratitude

theft, 148–149

theology, xiv, 41, 52, 53, 57, 59–61, 190, 214–215

Thomas Aquinas, St., 59

thought(s), 5, 9, 42–43, 44, 59, 73–74, 113, 202. *See also* conscience; doubt

time: beginning of, 73, 75, 81, 170 (*see also* creation; evolution); end of, 74, 76, 79, 83, 93, 166, 171, 179–180, 182, 210

Tondrakianism, **31**

Totemism, **18**

Tractarian Movement, 37

Tradition, 58, 59, 63–64, 72, 99, 123, 124, 214, 228

Traditionalism. *See* Fideism

transcendence, 47

Transgenderism, **62**, 72, 152, 177, 228

transgression, 45, 141. *See also* sin(s)

Transhumanism, **64**, **69–70**, 72

Transmigrationism. *See* Reincarnationism

transubstantiation, 33, 35, 40, 118, 119, 120, **229**–230

trial(s), 8–9, 181

trust, 138, 139, 180, 214

Truth(s), 48, 50–51, 53, 59, 67, 69, 73, 86, 87, 100, 102, 108, 110, 112, 118, 152, 155, 181, 214, 215; Declaration of, 216–233; God as source of, 75, 83–84, 86, 102, 108, 109, 114; neglect or rejection of revealed (*see* heresy; unbelief); offenses against, 54, 61, 63, 76–77, 85, 101, 109, 114, 122, 131, 144–145, 155–156, 188, 205, 206, 211

tyranny, 71, 148

U

unbelief, 60, 83, 85, 101, 108, 166–167, 172, 173

unction, extreme (*see* anointing of the sick)

understanding, 95, 98, 106, 137, 173–174, 187, 229

union: body-soul, 72, 151, 151n168; of the Church's members, 56, 87–90, 102, 122, 160, 223; with God, 38, 110, 178 (*see also* sanctifying grace); hypostatic (*see* Jesus Christ: fully God and fully man); of spouses (*see* marriage)

Unitarianism, **41**, 68

unity, 122, 159, 217; of all men in Adam, 73, 141; of the divine nature, 68, 84, 84n73; mark of the Church (*see under* mark[s] of the Church)

Universalism, 22, 23, 74, 80–81, 224

universe, 14, 16, 20, 41, 68–69, 71, 188

V

vaccines, 148–149
Valentinianism, **21**
value(s), 55, 56, 59, 80, 84n71, 150, 172
veneration, 30, 33, 40, 85, 119, 121, 136, 144, 180–181
venial sin, 139–140
vernacular, 58, 158–159
vessels, sacred, 120, 166
Vicar of Christ. *See* Supreme Pontiff
vice(s), 143, 156, 167–168
victim, 119, 230–231. *See also* sacrifice(s)
victory, 169, 176–177, 179, 181, 183–184
vigilance, 174, 210, 216, 218–219
vine, 6
violence, 35, 51, 130, 132–133, 148, 179, 180. *See also* killing
virginity, 26, 79, 176, 182–182; of the Blessed Virgin Mary, perpetual, 19, 26, 165, 172, 182–183, 184
virtue(s), 7, 48, 54, 92, 108, 111, 112, 173. *See also individual virtues*
Vision of God (Beatific). *See* Beatific Vision
voice(s), 93–94, 121, 158–159, 183, 219
vow(s), 48, 197, 201

W

wage(s), 179
Waldensianism, **33**
war(s), 31, 32, 34–35, 153, 156, 165–166, 176–177, 180–184, 217–218
weakness, 71, 120
weapons, 176
wedding, 145. *See also* marriage
Wesleyanism. *See* Methodism
widow(s), 128
wife. *See* marriage
will: of angels, 70; of Christ, 29, 77, 231, 232–233; divine, 28, 61, 63, 70, 74, 79, 83–84, 113, 122, 152, 169, 224; of man (*see* free will)
wine, 118, 229–230
wisdom, 152, 156, 157, 167, 172, 178
witchcraft, 15, 61, 144
witness(es), 67, 120, 160, 177, 179, 180, 206, 217–218, 232
wizardry, 15
woman/women, ineligible for holy orders, 122–124, 177–178. *See also* Feminism
Word of God: Incarnate. *See* Jesus Christ; Scripture as, 81, 226; in the Trinity, 223
words, 13, 64, 76, 93, 138, 161, 165, 168, 176–177, 209, 215, 230–231. *See also* language(s); semantics
work. *See* labor
works: good, 47, 80, 108, 110, 139, 142; of mercy, 139
world, 15, 16, 30, 32, 34, 44, 54, 56, 62, 68, 83–84, 139, 143, 165–174, 183, 188, 222; end of (*see under* time)
worship: false, 81–82, 84, 84n71, 91, 110, 135–139, **144**–146, 202, 224 (*see also* Freemasonry; religion: false); public official (*see* liturgy); true, retained in the Church alone (*see under* one)
wrath, God's, 85
Wycliffism, 34–**35**

Y

Yoga, 59, 110, 136, 137–138
youth, 196–197. *See also* children

Z

zeal, 5–6, 137
Zwinglianism, 39, **41**, 118

About the Author

BISHOP ATHANASIUS SCHNEIDER is one of the foremost defenders of Catholic orthodoxy today. He is a prolific author and serves as auxiliary bishop of the Archdiocese of St. Mary in Astana, Kazakhstan, chairman of the Liturgical Commission, and secretary-general of the Conference of Catholic Bishops of Kazakhstan. He is the author of many books, including *The Springtime That Never Came*, *The Catholic Mass*, and the most current and engaging catechism of our time, *Credo: Compendium of the Catholic Faith*.

Sophia Institute

Sophia Institute is a nonprofit institution that seeks to nurture the spiritual, moral, and cultural life of souls and to spread the gospel of Christ in conformity with the authentic teachings of the Roman Catholic Church.

Sophia Institute Press fulfills this mission by offering translations, reprints, and new publications that afford readers a rich source of the enduring wisdom of mankind.

Sophia Institute also operates the popular online resource CatholicExchange.com. *Catholic Exchange* provides world news from a Catholic perspective as well as daily devotionals and articles that will help readers to grow in holiness and live a life consistent with the teachings of the Church.

In 2013, Sophia Institute launched Sophia Institute for Teachers to renew and rebuild Catholic culture through service to Catholic education. With the goal of nurturing the spiritual, moral, and cultural life of souls, and an abiding respect for the role and work of teachers, we strive to provide materials and programs that are at once enlightening to the mind and ennobling to the heart; faithful and complete, as well as useful and practical.

Sophia Institute gratefully recognizes the Solidarity Association for preserving and encouraging the growth of our apostolate over the course of many years. Without their generous and timely support, this book would not be in your hands.

www.SophiaInstitute.com
www.CatholicExchange.com
www.SophiaInstituteforTeachers.org

Sophia Institute Press is a registered trademark of Sophia Institute. Sophia Institute is a tax-exempt institution as defined by the Internal Revenue Code, Section 501(c)(3). Tax ID 22-2548708.